1,825 DAYS OF HELL: ONE MAN'S ODYSSEY THROUGH THE AMERICAN PAROLE SYSTEM

1,825 DAYS OF HELL: ONE MAN'S ODYSSEY THROUGH THE AMERICAN PAROLE SYSTEM

Corrupt and Self-Propagating US Correctional System

JERRY TANNER

Copyright © 2014 Jerry Tanner.

All rights reserved. No part of this book may be used or reproduced by any means, graphic, electronic, or mechanical, including photocopying, recording, taping or by any information storage retrieval system without the written permission of the publisher except in the case of brief quotations embodied in critical articles and reviews.

Balboa Press books may be ordered through booksellers or by contacting:

Balboa Press
A Division of Hay House
1663 Liberty Drive
Bloomington, IN 47403
www.balboapress.com
1 (877) 407-4847

Because of the dynamic nature of the Internet, any web addresses or links contained in this book may have changed since publication and may no longer be valid. The views expressed in this work are solely those of the author and do not necessarily reflect the views of the publisher, and the publisher hereby disclaims any responsibility for them.

The author of this book does not dispense medical advice or prescribe the use of any technique as a form of treatment for physical, emotional, or medical problems without the advice of a physician, either directly or indirectly. The intent of the author is only to offer information of a general nature to help you in your quest for emotional and spiritual well-being. In the event you use any of the information in this book for yourself, which is your constitutional right, the author and the publisher assume no responsibility for your actions.

Any people depicted in stock imagery provided by Thinkstock are models, and such images are being used for illustrative purposes only. Certain stock imagery © Thinkstock.

Printed in the United States of America.

ISBN: 978-1-4525-2094-0 (sc)
ISBN: 978-1-4525-2095-7 (e)

Library of Congress Control Number: 2014915265

Balboa Press rev. date: 8/22/2014

CONTENTS

Prologue vii

Chapter 1: Released on Parole, Anchorage 1
    Like a Punch in the Face 1
    Making Plans 7

Chapter 2: Going through the Motions 21
    The Monotony of Days 21
    Old "Friends" 24

Chapter 3: A Jail without Bars 39
    Anchored Down 39
    Nothing but Roadblocks 43

Chapter 4: Deliverance Delayed 51
    Bureaucratic Bullshit 51
    Life Goes On 56

Chapter 5: Be Careful What You Wish For 65
    Leaving Alaska 65
    You Can't Go Home Again 67
    Out of the Frying Pan... 69

...And Out of the Workplace 79
   A Moot Point 83
   The Casinos Become my Refuge 89

Chapter 6: When Enough Becomes Too Much 93
   Revelations and Coming to Terms 93
   A Night on the Town 98

Chapter 7: My Book: Banned in Ohio 105
   A Reason for Being 105
   Let the Buzz Begin! 113
   The Game Comes to an End 122

Chapter 8: Conclusion 137
   The Failure of the Promise of Parole and
      Probation as Vehicles of Reentry 137
   A Hard Look at U.S. Prison and Parole Statistics 144
   The Challenges to Reentry 147
   Housing 148
   Employment 151
   A Corrupted System 156

Epilogue 161

PROLOGUE

In my book *Derailed* I gave a general autobiographical accounting of my life up until I went to prison in Alaska; or, more accurately, up until the time I was released from prison in Alaska. That is, the first time I was released from prison in Alaska. I had been sent to jail as the result of a plea bargain. I did not commit the crime I was accused of, and, what I had actually done was no crime at all. I took the plea deal because my legal team was utterly convinced that I could not get a fair trial, here, in America. And I faced a much stiffer penalty if I fought for my innocence against a prosecutor more interested in winning convictions than serving justice, and in front of a judge more interested in showing herself as a tough-on-crime conservative than in examining, objectively, the merits of the case in front of an unbiased jury, while at the same time lacking enough humbleness to allow my case to be sent to a court, and a jury, that could. And the latter are also the reasons, I believe, that my attorneys' request for a change of venue was also denied.

In the years before my incarceration I had been a successful businessman; highly successful, in fact. In the state of Alaska I had launched a health care company from scratch in 1999 and grew it to over $20 million in annual revenues in less than seven years; in the state of Maine, at the urging of the Governor himself, I had taken over a mail order pharmacy that was bankrupt and riddled with corruption, whose executive leaders were allegedly embezzling millions of dollars, and completely transformed it, in the space of a year within which it was making $2.7 million *monthly*. Most important to me, these were good, humanly worthwhile businesses that provided vital services of essential health care and prescription medicines that helped many thousands of people live better lives, and to be able to enjoy their lives just a little bit more. From very early in my life, from the time I had started up a small pet shop in my home town, and took over a bar in a nearby town, I had shown a knack for business. In fact, over my lifetime I was told many times informally by friends and associates, years before it actually appeared "officially," in print in the major newspapers covering the states of Alaska and Maine, that I have a natural born entrepreneurial talent; that my core skill is opening and starting up, managing, and effectively growing new business ventures. What I have far less of a knack for, apparently, is judging or expecting the dishonest, nasty, and downright despicable things that people are willing to do to you, even those who claim to be your partners in business or in life. And I was tragically, hopelessly naïve about what our cherished legal system is willing to do to a person. Heretofore, I had actually believed that the American Justice System was there to protect the innocent. How wrong had I been!

After my plea deal, I was forced to remove myself from Immediate Care, the multi-million dollar health care company I founded and built in Alaska, because, now "officially" a felon, I was no longer entitled to hold contracts with the State of Alaska, for human services, or anything else for that matter. While in prison, I could do nothing but watch helplessly as my former partner usurped control, and eventually ownership, of I-Care Pharmacy, the multi-million dollar mail-order prescription service in Maine that I had resurrected from bankruptcy, with, I might add, the aid of my own attorneys, who dragged out the proceedings and bled me dry in the process, and who often seemed more on my partner's side than on mine. But then, I guess you go where the money is going.

Notwithstanding, this book is not about self-pity, or how I was "done wrong" and didn't deserve it. As depressed and demoralized as I might have been on the worst days in prison, when my time had been served and I was released in the summer of 2009, I knew that I wanted to get my life back. I knew it would be difficult to put everything that had happened behind me and move forward, and I knew it would be very difficult to start over from scratch, no longer a kid who believed he could do anything, but I also knew I would eventually one day summon the courage to do what my Uncle Roger, the retired Air Force officer had urged me to do: "You need to get back into the business world because that's what you're good at," he had said, "That's your passion! You need to get back in there and be a part of society again!"

The day of my release finally came, and as I related the story in *Derailed*, on that day I told all of my esteemed inmate colleagues that if they ever wanted to see me again, they'd have to do it "on the outside" because, as I said to them, "I ain't never comin' back here!" That would turn out to be false. Because on the day of my release, when I stepped out of a DOC mini-bus onto the streets of Anchorage along with a handful of other, bewildered former inmates, I thought, naïve once again to a fault, that the lion's share of my troubles—the ramifications of following my attorneys advice instead of my own heart's desire to fight for what was right—would be over.

Nothing could have been further from the truth.

As I mentioned earlier, *Derailed*, my first book, is the story of my life up until the day I was released on parole from the minimum security prison in Alaska known as Palmer Correctional Center, give or take a few months. In August of 2012, that book was featured in an Advocate.com article titled, "21 LGBT Biographies or Memoirs You Should Read Now." This book is the story of the remarkable things, both good and bad, that have happened in the aftermath.

CHAPTER 1
RELEASED ON PAROLE, ANCHORAGE

Like a Punch in the Face

Being carted off to jail, or prison, call it what you will, feels like a deep, bloodless wound when you know in your heart that you committed no criminal offense, not to mention knowing in the plain rationality of your mind that you are innocent of even so much as having the intent to commit any wrongdoing at all, much less a bona fide crime. I don't know how actual criminals feel about it—the ones who had committed burglaries and car thefts, or had drug convictions or other offenses that were just serious enough to land them in minimum-security Palmer, but not serious enough to send them to a more restrictive facility—but I can only judge that for them, being incarcerated from time to time was simply a part of that life. I actually and honestly mean them no disrespect, nor certainly not to condemn them for this. In truth, the only basis I have for making such a judgment was the cavalier and casual way that some of the inmates at PCC seemed to take being "inside" in stride. There were, for instance, those times when a "new" inmate would walk into the common area and be cheerfully greeted and welcomed back with laughter and high-fives from the inmates already in residence like it was some sort of family reunion. So many of those guys had been there before, and they all seemed to be great buddies who knew each other rather well. And make no mistake about it, as much as law enforcement and department of corrections officials publically decry the high recidivism rates across the country, the fact of the matter is that the criminal justice and correctional systems in virtually all 50 states rely on the revolving door of recidivism for their continued existence, funding, job security and growth.

While I was in PCC, I had resolved to get through it, to behave, follow the rules, and do my time; get released and then go about rebuilding my life. But when I got out, that bloodless wound was still there—it is a wound to the psyche, not to the physical body (though it can take its toll there too, as stress so often does). Being released from prison was one of the strangest and most awkward feelings I have ever experienced in my life. As much as you are expecting it to be a kind of cathartic release, it actually puts a person into a state of paranoia. You go around feeling branded, as if you are wearing a big black barcode imprinted into your forehead that says "EX-CON." You go around expecting that people will recognize you as a criminal: "Hey, there's the guy who just spent 16 months in Palmer Correctional Center! What's he doing here?" You literally "feel" like a social pariah, and I found this as troubling and as hurtful as it was remarkable, because heretofore I would have never imagined that being a "social pariah" could actually have a specific feeling associated with it. And further, all that I had ever done previously in my personal and business life was to try to help people.

And life as an "ex-con" makes you flinch, almost literally, as though, when you try to go out to public places and lead a normal life, life itself is going to punch you in the face for no reason other than the fact that you once went to prison, never mind why, or whether you were truly guilty of anything or actually deserved to go there in the first place. An overheard conversation in a restaurant, an odd look from someone on the street, each makes you wonder: are they talking about me, or, what was that look all about? So you go about your day feeling like you have to look over your shoulder all the time. I know that's irrational, and maybe a bit of paranoia, but that's how you feel, and it's a big part of the hurt that you feel.

Back during the days and months leading up to my trial, and when things seemed to be spiraling out of control, was when I had first gotten the notion that I ought to write a book about my experiences, and about the things that were happening to me in life and business that I seemed utterly powerless to stop or get control of in any appreciable way. Somewhere along the way, someone suggested that I should start keeping a daily diary or journal in which to write down everything that was happening so that I'd have a written record, and wouldn't forget anything. I didn't dare try to do such a thing in prison for fear of reprisals from the corrections officers who might think that I was writing down bad things about them. I don't know whether or not that was unjustified paranoia on my part, perhaps from watching too many gangster movies or police dramas on TV. I suppose I was being melodramatic.

Still, there was the incident, recounted in *Derailed*, when my attorney, unbeknownst to me, tried to slip a tape recorder and twelve blank cassette tapes past the guards responsible for checking through our incoming mail for contraband, which was the only time I got into any hot water with the corrections officers, including being dragged to an appearance before one of the sergeants and then ultimately the Camp Commandant himself, who, shall I say, was rather cross about it until I was able to convince him that my intentions were in no way sinister. My attorney had gotten quite a kick out of hearing about that little confrontation, but I didn't find it particularly amusing. Still, keeping a written journal in jail, where it's pretty darn difficult to conceal anything that you're doing, might have put me much more at risk with the other inmates than with the corrections officers or their superiors. Whether or not there is any such thing as "honor among thieves," one thing that my jailhouse colleagues seemed to universally hate and despise was a "snitch." If any of these guys had gotten the slightest whim of an idea that I was writing down stuff about *them* or their crimes, I would have been subject to unmerciful and unrelenting abuse by the whole lot of them, while the guards would ignore their actions or simply look the other way (and probably gain some not-so-secret sadistic pleasure from observing it going on). Regardless, I thought that the idea of writing my thoughts and activities down in a daily journal was a good one, and I started to do precisely that, immediately, on Day One of my freedom, June 28th, 2009 when I was released from PCC onto the streets of Anchorage, and collected there by my Mom and Dad.

There is perhaps nothing that better illuminates the vacuity of my mental state, the painful depression and emotional exhaustion I felt, and the desperate desire to withdraw into myself, all of which 16 months behind prison walls had put me in, than the first 30 or 40 daily entries in that journal from July to mid-August, the summer of 2009. Most of those entries are one-liners, and they curtly describe watching TV one day, playing cards the next, and on the more adventurous occasions, taking a walk outside or maybe risking a single trip to Wal-Mart or some such place. Many of them say simply and nonspecifically, "Stayed at home with the family." It's true that my family was there for me and there really wasn't much that I had to do that they couldn't do for me if necessary, if I simply didn't feel up to it—outside of reporting immediately to my parole officer of course—and I was desperately grateful they were there. If they weren't, I probably would have rolled up in a ball on the floor of my Anchorage apartment and stayed there until I starved to death. Getting out of prison, I learned, is not some wondrous, miraculous event of striding back into freedom and into the light of some new day, there is no veil of sorrow and darkness that is lifted, no "great weight" that is removed from one's shoulders. In hindsight, I would have to say there are few, if any, occasions in life that are more anticlimactic than being released from jail! And for me in particular there was, at best, only the lingering anxiety and the unresolved issue of what I was going to do with the rest of my life now, now that I had lost one of my companies and was engaged in a bitter battle over the other, which was not likely to end well for me, either. The only thing I was sure of was that I wanted to go home to Ohio and be with my family while I sorted things out.

And if my principal reason for wanting to go home to Ohio was an emotional-psychological one, and in some sense a non-rational one (I say non-rational deliberately as opposed to irrational, because my desire to go back was certainly not "irrational) of simply wanting to be with the only people I felt I could trust anymore, that being my family of course, there were in fact some sound practical, rational (or semi-rational!) reasons for wanting to do so as well. For one thing, I had lost my business in Alaska, and it had happened in something of a public disgrace in that the story of my indictment, trial, and sentencing had made the papers. It wasn't the bad publicity that bothered me—by now that had been nearly two years earlier, and I doubted, in my clearer moments, that anyone would remember that far back, or that they would care about all of that anymore, for that matter. But with

Immediate Care gone, there was really nothing to keep me in Alaska anymore. I was prohibited from working in the health care industry that I loved by virtue of now being a convicted felon and thus no longer allowed to be a party to state health care contracts. Nor would the local bankers or financial institutions have anything to do with me after what had happened.

But another reason I think I wanted to get out of Alaska was that I felt railroaded by a state that for all intents and purposes refused to give me the opportunity for a fair trial in which to air my side of the story, a state that effectively denied me due process under the law, and ultimately denied me justice. I wanted to leave Alaska at least in part because I felt that the state had screwed me over—big time. Whether that's a "rational" reason or not, well, I simply don't care. What Alaska did to me was despicable, plain and simple. If, after all of that, I wanted out of the state, who could blame me?

So in any case, and as required, I reported in to the parole office on the first full day after my release, June 29th, whereupon I was told that reporting in was merely an intake procedure, and I was set up to meet my PO, one Greg Matthews, nine days later on July 8th. At that first face-to-face meeting, I informed Mr. Matthews that I wanted to immediately initiate a formal request for transfer to the state of Ohio. PO Matthews told me that the procedure involved to do that would take up to 45 days to complete. It was the first of a legion of falsehoods, half-truths, and out-and-out lies that I would be told by law enforcement and corrections officials over the entire frustrating course of the time I would remain on parole. It was also my first lesson in learning that being released from prison does not mean you are now free—not by a long shot.

Making Plans

As demoralized as I might have been, I was determined to get back to work doing something productive when I got out. In the heyday of Immediate Care in Alaska and I-Care Pharmacy clear across the continent in Maine, I had, at times, been working 70-hour weeks and, I confess, loving it. Admittedly, my former life partner did not love it, and he would claim that my dedication to my work was one of the main factors contributing to our breakup, but I never believed that line of bull from him anyway. Besides, a lot of water had gone under that bridge by now, and I had a strong sense that I should try to get busy again if I wanted to retain my sanity.

While I was in PCC, I had asked one of my attorneys to research book publishers and literary agents, and as soon as I was released I started to contact each and every one of them to see if I could find one who would be interested in publishing my story. I also set to work writing it, even going so far as hiring an editor to help with conceptualizing and developing the manuscript in order to make sure it met publisher-worthy professional standards for style and content. In addition, as soon as I was out, I started researching different businesses that I might like to get into. In particular, I looked at numerous franchise opportunities. I reasoned that I wasn't a "kid" anymore, I didn't know if I still had the energy and brashness to start a new company from scratch, and really, I guess I was honest enough with myself to realize that I just didn't want to go through that whole start-up ordeal again, having been through it more than once before. So a time-tested and "proven" franchise seemed like a good way to go if I could find one that I really liked. I also decided that getting some serious exercise would be a good way to try to ward off depression, and perhaps relieve some of the boredom that I had experienced in jail, and which I expected to continue on the "outside" until such time as I could find something useful to busy myself with. So about a month after my release I joined the Alaska Club, a fitness and exercise organization with a location in South Anchorage, which I visited pretty regularly for the first several months.

My parents stayed in Anchorage with me in as long as they could, but eventually it would be time for them to go home to Ohio. They stayed through July, and flew home on the 31st. I was very sad to see them go, and they were worried for me, worried about leaving me alone up there. But I told them I'd be fine, and actually, I wouldn't be alone right away, because about a week and a half prior to their leaving, my Uncle Roger had arrived in town, and the two of us would pal around for another week or so, that is until he too had to head home. So I think that made it a little easier for my parents to more or less "hand me off" to Uncle Roger when we said our good-bye's at the airport. Uncle Roger was a retired Air Force officer, and he loved to go out to Elmendorf Air Force base and kick around a bit. He had planned to stay in Anchorage for a few weeks into August, but then some important family business forced him to cut short his stay, and he left on the 6th. I chauffeured him to the airport, and when the plane took off, for the first time since I had met Russell Stoner almost 20 years earlier, I was alone and on my own in Alaska. It was like the words of that old Michelle Shocked song; I was "anchored down in Anchorage." Only the "anchor" was the Alaska Department of Corrections.

But by that time, I was pretty much okay with it, or at minimum, I was resigned to the fact that it had become clear that my situation was going to be that way for an indeterminate amount of time. Because, just a few days prior to my parents' departure, in just my second meeting with PO Greg Matthews, he had told me that my initial request for transfer to Ohio had been denied. As it turned out, I was in part responsible for this rejection because, when I was released from Palmer, I had refused to sign off on the "Conditions of Mandatory Parole," which, ironically enough, I was required to abide by whether I signed off on them or not. However, I had done this on *the advice of counsel.* The Alaska Order of Mandatory Parole unequivocally states that (quoting verbatim), "The Parole Board may have me returned to custody at any time when it determines that a condition of parole has been violated." One has to wonder why the state even bothers to give the individual parolee the option to sign the conditions at all, given that it makes no difference whatsoever whether you do or don't, but there you go! It's also interesting to note in passing that the statement says "when" a condition of parole has been violated, rather than "if." Not a particularly optimistic or fair-minded attitude on the part of the Parole Board, which seems to regard parole violations as inevitable.

Later in this book, I will have much, much more to say about the restrictions embodied in the "Conditions of Mandatory Parole," and particularly the *much longer* list of "Supplemental Conditions of Mandatory Parole." (See Figures 1A through 1F at the end of this chapter.) And worse still are the restrictions that are not specifically defined under the conditions of parole that the parole board may impose arbitrarily, and without cause or reasonable explanation, but simply at the board's discretionary whim, and against which no legal means of appeal exists, which I will also discuss at length. However, because my refusal to sign came back to bite me in the ass so quickly after my release to prevent me from doing the one thing, perhaps the only thing, that I was certain I wanted to do, which was to go home to Ohio, it is perhaps necessary to briefly explain here why I had refused, which I had done both on principle and, as I stated earlier, on the advice of counsel. Rather than some act of grandiose defiance, the principle aspect of it was, on the most basic level, a matter of simple, logical practicality, and I can use just one simple "condition" of parole as an example to illustrate this.

Specifically, provision 32 of the "Supplemental Conditions" would have prohibited me not only from consuming or having alcoholic beverages "in my possession," it also would have prohibited me from going into establishments where alcoholic beverages were served. I naturally took this to include any restaurants that had a liquor license. After all, my attorney told me quite bluntly that, in essence, "If you sign off on those conditions, the parole board will hold you right to the letter of each provision," such that, for example, I would risk being in violation of my parole if one fine morning I bought a cup of coffee, a doughnut, and a lottery ticket at a deli that also sold beer. I felt strongly that this was totally unfair, and moreover, had absolutely nothing to do with the things I was charged with in the first place. There were a number of conditions just like this, which imposed prohibitions against a whole wash-list of things that had nothing to do with me, or with my case, and which I therefore believed (and still do) should never have been applied to me. So I refused to sign, and I turned the whole matter over to my attorneys to resolve. They, of course, failed, and the state refused to budge.

That, however, was only the State of Alaska's contribution to the rejection of my transfer application. The State of Ohio also had to be heard from, and it turned out that Ohio's DOC had also rejected the transfer, and on equally ridiculous grounds. My paperwork had indicated that I planned to move back into a beautiful, 4,000 square-foot home on Center Street in Ashland, not far from my parents, which I still owned. I had bought the house in 2007 before all of this happened, so that I would have a place to stay when visiting my parents, which I had planned, or at least expected, to do more often because they were getting older and beginning to experience health issues. I had wanted to be able to help them out when they needed me. But Ohio had discovered that there was a church nearby that home which ran a small daycare. You can see where this is going. There were no less than three provisions in the "Supplemental Conditions of Mandatory Parole" that strictly—and I would add, vehemently—prohibited me from having contact with minors in any way (Number 21: NO CONTACT WITH PERSONS UNDER 18 YEARS OLD; Number 22: MAY NOT RESIDE IN HOUSEHOLD WITH PERSON UNDER 18 YEARS OLD; and Number 29: MAY NOT ENGAGE IN ANY EMPLOYMENT OR VOLUNTEER ACTIVITY THAT INVOLVES CONTACT WITH MINORS UNDER THE AGE OF 18).

Here again, certainly—absolutely—none of this nonsense had any connection whatsoever to the crime I was alleged to have committed. Moreover, I can think of nothing in this world more abhorrent than child sex abuse or pedophilia. But what made these "conditions" of parole ever so much more intensely hurtful to me was the fact that I was a victim of just such abuse as a child and as a young teenager. Regardless, under Ohio's rules, the church-based daycare facility was simply too close to my home for them to allow me to live there (though none of the three parole conditions detailed earlier actually specifies exactly what an "appropriate" or permissible distance to the nearest daycare center actually ought to be!). So now I faced either hiring (and paying lavishly) yet another lawyer in Ohio to fight this latest insult, not simply to my dignity—I could swallow that—but to my humanity, or I could resign myself to selling a home I loved and cherished, and simply buy another someplace where I wouldn't be seen as a threat to little children by the state of Ohio.

Perhaps, then, I shouldn't have been surprised when PO Matthews informed me in our meeting in late July that my transfer was denied. I must admit, however, that Greg was really very good about it, even showing a little bit of compassion. He suggested that I try again, but of course this time I would probably have to sign the Conditions of Parole statements. We went over the transfer papers together, and he said that he would go ahead and begin the process to resubmit the application to the parole board, for which I was thankful. And I settled in, reluctantly, for what I now suspected was going to be a long fight to get my transfer approved. (See Figure 2 at the end of this chapter.)

ALASKA BOARD OF PAROLE

ORDER OF MANDATORY PAROLE

Parolee __TANNER, Jerry L.__ DOB __07/27/1961__ Released __06/28/2009__ Supv. Expires __02/27/2010__

The following terms and conditions are effective on the release date shown on the CERTIFICATE OF GOOD TIME AWARD (AS 33.20.030) for all prisoners released pursuant to AS 33.16.010(a) or AS 33.20.040. I understand I am required by law to abide by the conditions imposed, whether or not I sign these conditions. The Parole Board may have me returned to custody at any time when it determines a condition of parole has been violated.

CONDITIONS OF MANDATORY PAROLE

1. **REPORT UPON RELEASE:** I will report in person no later than the next working day after my release to the P.O. located at __Anchorage, AK__ and receive further reporting instructions.

2. **MAINTAIN EMPLOYMENT/TRAINING/TREATMENT:** I will make a diligent effort to maintain steady employment and support my legal dependents. I will not voluntarily change or terminate employment without receiving permission from my Parole Officer (P.O.) to do so. If discharged or if employment is terminated (temporarily or permanently) for any reason, I will notify my P.O. the next working day. If I am involved in an education, training or treatment program, I will continue active participation in the program unless I receive permission from my P.O. to quit. If I am released, removed or terminated from the program for any reason, I will notify my P.O. the next working day.

3. **REPORT MONTHLY:** I will report to my P.O. at least monthly in the manner prescribed by my P.O. I will follow any other reporting instructions established by my P.O. My P.O. may require me to report as often as deemed necessary.

4. **OBEY LAWS/ORDERS:** I will obey all state, federal and local laws, ordinances, orders, and court orders.

5. **PERMISSION BEFORE CHANGING RESIDENCE:** I will obtain permission from my P.O. before changing my residence. Remaining away from my approved residence for 24 hours or more constitutes a change in residence for the purpose of this condition.

6. **TRAVEL PERMIT BEFORE TRAVEL OUTSIDE ALASKA:** I will obtain the prior written permission of my P.O. in the form of an interstate travel agreement before leaving the State of Alaska. Failure to abide by the conditions of the travel agreement is a violation of my order of parole.

7. **NO FIREARMS / WEAPONS:** I will not own, possess, have in my custody, handle, purchase or transport any firearm, ammunition or explosives. I may not carry any deadly weapon on my person except a pocket knife with a 3" or shorter blade. Carrying any other weapon on my person such as a hunting knife, axe, club, etc. is a violation of my order of parole. I will contact the Alaska Board of Parole if I have any questions about the use of firearms, ammunition or weapons.

8. **NO DRUGS:** I will not use, possess, handle, purchase, give or administer any narcotic, hallucinogenic (including marijuana/THC), stimulant, depressant, amphetamine, barbiturate or prescription drug not specifically prescribed by a licensed medical professional.

9. **REPORT POLICE CONTACT:** I will report to my P.O., not later than the next working day, any contact with a law enforcement officer.

10. **DO NOT WORK AS AN INFORMANT:** I will not enter into any agreement or other arrangement with any law enforcement agency which will place me in the position of violating any law or any condition of my parole. I understand that Department of Corrections and Parole Board policy prohibit me from working as an informant in any manner and in any degree.

11. **NO CONTACT WITH PRISONERS OR FELONS:** I may not telephone, correspond with or visit any person confined in a prison, penitentiary, correctional institution or camp, jail, halfway house, work release center, community residential center, juvenile correctional center, etc. Contact with a felon during the course of employment or during Corrections-related treatment is not prohibited if approved by my P.O. Any other knowing contact with a felon is prohibited unless approved by my P.O. I will notify my P.O. the next working day if I have contact with a prisoner or felon.

12. **CANNOT LEAVE AREA:** I will receive permission from my P.O. before leaving the area of the state to which my case is assigned. My P.O. will advise me in writing of limits to the area to which I have been assigned.

13. **OBEY ALL ORDERS / SPECIAL CONDITIONS:** I will obey any special instructions, rules or orders given to me by the Board of Parole or by my P.O. and I will follow any special or additional conditions imposed by the Board of Parole or my P.O.

14. **WAIVE EXTRADITION:** I will waive extradition to the State of Alaska from any state or territory of the United States, and I will not contest efforts to return me to Alaska by the Board of Parole or my P.O.

15. **PROVIDE DNA SAMPLE:** I will provide a blood and/or oral sample when requested by a health care professional acting on behalf of the State, if I am being released after a conviction of an offense requiring the State to collect the sample(s) for the DNA identification system under AS 44.41.035.

I have received a copy of these conditions of parole. I have had the opportunity to read these conditions or to have them read to me if I cannot read. My mandatory parole can be revoked and I can be required to serve the remainder of my sentence if I violate any parole conditions. I understand it is my responsibility to contact my P.O. if I have a question about the meaning or intent of any parole condition. I realize I can be arrested by a P.O. at any time with or without a warrant if my conduct so dictates. I understand that I am required by law to abide by the conditions imposed, whether or not I sign these conditions.

__Refused to sign__   __5/19/09__
Parolee signature   Date   Witness Signature   Title

Printed Name of Witness

Alaska Board of Parole, 550 West 7th Ave., Ste # 601, Anchorage, AK 99501
Rev. 3/08; Alaska Board of Parole [g:\parole\forms\Standard MR Cond.doc]

FIG 1A-E. My "Conditions of Mandatory Parole"

Alaska Board of Parole
SUPPLEMENTAL CONDITIONS OF MANDATORY PAROLE
2

TANNER, Jerry L.   CASE#3PA-S07-00316CR.

16. **REPORT UPON ARRIVAL:** I will report to the supervising parole officer the next working day after arrival in the state in which I will be supervised.

17. **FOLLOW INTERSTATE CONDITIONS:** I understand I am obligated to abide by the conditions of parole established by the Alaska Board of Parole, as well as the conditions of the state where I will be supervised. I understand the receiving state parole officer may set up any additional conditions that the parole officer finds necessary. Only the Alaska Board of Parole has the authority to change a condition of the Order of Parole from the Alaska Board of Parole.

18. **TRAVEL PERMIT REQUIRED BEFORE LEAVING RECEIVING STATE:** I will not leave the state where I am being supervised without the prior permission of my receiving state's parole officer, including an Interstate Travel Permit.

19. **ALASKA RESIDENCY UNTIL INTERSTATE TRANSFER APPROVED:** Until such time as my interstate parole transfer occurs I must reside either in: (a) a community where a Parole Officer is assigned or (b) in a community where a Parole Officer is not assigned but where I have obtained a community contact person who is approved by my Parole Officer. I understand that my Parole Officer will provide appropriate notification to the community where I will reside. If my interstate transfer is not approved, I understand that I may appeal to the Board of Parole for modification to my residency conditions.

20. **RESIDENCE:** I will reside in a community where I am able to obtain recommended *SUBSTANCE ABUSE / SEX OFFENDER* treatment or programs which are imposed as a condition of my parole. If I am unable to obtain such treatment or programs but I am on a waiting list for treatment, my Parole Officer may authorize me to reside temporarily in a different location, but only until my treatment or programs become available to me. If I reside in a community where a Parole Officer is not assigned, I will obtain a community contact person approved by my Parole Officer. After I am treatment complete or program complete, I may reside in a community where a Parole Officer is not assigned but where I have obtained a community contact person who is approved by my Parole Officer. I understand that my Parole Officer will provide appropriate notification to the community where I will reside.

21. **NO CONTACT WITH PERSONS UNDER 18 YEARS OLD:** I will not knowingly have any in-person contact with a person under 18 years old unless I am in the immediate presence of another adult who knows the circumstances of my crime (including the assault cycle of my crime, if appropriate) and this adult has been approved by my parole officer. My parole officer must provide prior written permission for contact to occur. This restriction regarding in-person contact with minors includes employment, recreational and residential situations, unless the contact with a minor has been approved in writing by the Alaska Board of Parole. This restriction does not prohibit incidental contact in public locations. The restriction does not prohibit conversations in public with a minor employee of a business. Contact includes but is not limited to no in-person contact, no written correspondence, no taped conversations, no electronic contact (internet or EMail), no telephonic contact, no stalking, no harassment and no communication of any nature through a third party, without the prior written permission of my parole officer.

I FULLY UNDERSTAND THAT THE CONDITIONS ON THIS PAGE HAVE THE SAME FORCE AND EFFECT AS THE STANDARD ORDER OF DISCRETIONARY PAROLE OR MANDATORY PAROLE AND ALL CONDITIONS LISTED ABOVE MUST BE FOLLOWED WHETHER I SIGN OR NOT.

Parolee: Refused to Sign

Dated: 5/10/09

Witness:

Title:

FIG. 1B

Alaska Board of Parole
SUPPLEMENTAL CONDITIONS OF MANDATORY PAROLE

TANNER, Jerry L.   CASE#3PA-S07-00316CR.

22. **MAY NOT RESIDE IN HOUSEHOLD WITH PERSON UNDER 18 YEARS OLD:** I will not reside in a dwelling in which a minor under the age of 18 years is residing or staying without the permission of my parole officer and my therapist (and parent/guardian of a minor).

23. **INFORM HOUSEHOLD MEMBERS OF CRIMINAL HISTORY:** I will advise all members of the household I am staying in of my criminal history. I understand my parole officer may discuss the circumstances of my criminal history with any household member.

24. **SEX OFFENDER EVALUATION:** I will obtain a sex offender evaluation from an approved provider to determine my need for sex offender monitoring / counseling / treatment. I will actively participate in an approved program as determined by the evaluation and participate in approved sex offender monitoring / counseling / treatment as directed by my parole officer. I will sign and abide by the conditions of a treatment agreement established by the treatment program. I will continue active participation and attendance in sex offender programming to my parole officer's satisfaction. I will obtain the prior permission of my parole officer before voluntarily discontinuing sex offender programming. If I am released, removed or terminated from this program (temporarily or permanently) for any reason, I will notify my parole officer the next working day. I agree to allow my parole officer access to any information obtained by the sex offender programming personnel, including my attendance and performance in the program.

25. **NO SEXUALLY EXPLICIT MATERIAL, AND SEARCH FOR MATERIALS:** I will not at any time possess or have on my person, in my computer, in my residence or in my car any sexually explicit material, including but no limited to: books, movies, videos, magazines, printed matter, computer disks or files. Upon request of a parole officer at any reasonable time, I will submit to a search of my person, my personal property, my residence, my vehicle or any vehicle under which I have control, for the presence of such material.

26. **CONTAINMENT MODEL PROGRAMMING:** I will actively, at the discretion of my Parole Officer, participate in Alaska Department of Corrections approved Containment Model Programming at my own expense. This program may include physiological and/or psychological assessment, testing, treatment and monitoring.

27. **POLYGRAPH TESTING:** I will participate in periodic polygraph testing at the direction of my parole officer.

28. **SEX OFFENDER ASSESSMENT/EVALUATION:** I will actively participate in Alaska Department of Corrections approved programming as determined by the Containment Model assessment/evaluation and I will participate in Containment Model programming as directed by my parole officer. I will sign and abide by the conditions of the treatment program included in the Containment Model program. I will continue active participation and attendance in the Alaska Department of Corrections approved Containment Model programming to my parole officer's satisfaction. I will obtain the prior permission of my parole officer before voluntarily discontinuing Containment Model programming. If I am released, removed or terminated from this program (temporarily or permanently) for any reason, I will notify my parole officer the next working day. I authorize the exchange of verbal and written information between the assessment provider, treatment provider, polygraph examiner and Alaska Department of Corrections staff members. Additionally, during the course of supervision and treatment, I authorize the exchange of information with other

I FULLY UNDERSTAND THAT THE CONDITIONS ON THIS PAGE HAVE THE SAME FORCE AND EFFECT AS THE STANDARD ORDER OF DISCRETIONARY PAROLE OR MANDATORY PAROLE AND ALL CONDITIONS LISTED ABOVE MUST BE FOLLOWED WHETHER I SIGN OR NOT.

Refused to Sign
Parolee

5/18/09
Dated

Witness

Title

FIG. 1C

Alaska Board of Parole
SUPPLEMENTAL CONDITIONS OF MANDATORY PAROLE

TANNER, Jerry L.   CASE#3PA-S07-00316CR.

individuals who are identified by Containment Model management team members as having an essential role in my supervision and treatment in the community

29. **MAY NOT ENGAGE IN ANY EMPLOYMENT OR VOLUNTEER COMMUNITY ACTIVITY THAT INVOLVES CONTACT WITH MINORS UNDER THE AGE OF EIGHTEEN:** I may not engage in any employment or volunteer activity that involves contact with minors under the age of eighteen years old, unless I am in the immediate presence of another adult who knows the circumstances of my crime (including the assault cycle of my crime, if appropriate) and this adult has been approved by my parole officer. My parole officer must provide prior written permission in order for contact to occur.

30. **SUBSTANCE ABUSE EVALUATION / TREATMENT / AFTERCARE / MONITORING:** I will have a recent substance abuse evaluation or will obtain one and will follow the recommendations of substance abuse treatment professionals. If recommended, I will actively participate in all approved substance abuse programming and aftercare as directed by my parole officer (which may include NA/AA). I will sign and abide by the conditions of a treatment agreement established by the treatment program. I will cooperate with program personnel and will sign the consent to release information as a criminal justice referral. I will continue active participation and attendance in substance abuse programming to my parole officer's satisfaction. I will obtain the prior permission of my parole officer before voluntarily discontinuing substance abuse programming. If I am released, removed or terminated from this programming (temporarily or permanently) for any reason, I will notify my parole officer the next working day. I agree to allow my parole officer access to any information obtained by substance abuse program personnel, including my attendance and performance in the program.

31. **SUBSTANCE ABUSE MONITORING:** I will enroll in and remain in any substance abuse monitoring program directed by my parole officer. I will cooperate with program personnel and will sign the consent to release confidential information as a criminal justice referral. I will obtain the prior permission of my parole officer before voluntarily discontinuing substance abuse monitoring. If I am released, removed or terminated from the program (temporarily or permanently) for any reason, I will notify my parole officer the next working day. I agree to allow my parole officer access to any information obtained by substance abuse program personnel, including my attendance and performance in the program.

32. **NO ALCOHOL CONSUMPTION / POSSESSION: ALCOHOL TESTING / SEARCH:** I will not consume or have in my possession at any time any alcoholic beverages, including "home brew." I will not enter an establishment in which the primary business is the dispensing of alcoholic beverages; this includes liquor stores, bars, pubs, taverns or night clubs. I will notify my parole officer the next working day after I use any prescription or over-the-counter drugs, or other substance containing alcohol. I will not at any time allow alcoholic beverages in my residence or in any motor vehicle I own or under which I have control. I will submit to testing at any reasonable time upon the request by or at the direction of a parole officer or peace officer to determine whether or not I have used alcoholic beverages. This testing includes, but is not limited to: blood test, breathalyzer, urinalysis. I understand that if any of these tests show that I have consumed alcoholic beverages, my parole may be revoked. Refusing to cooperate when requested to submit to testing will constitute a violation of this condition and may result in revocation of my parole. Upon request by or at the direction of a parole officer at any reasonable time, I will submit to a search of my person, my personal property, my residence, my vehicle, or any vehicle under which I have control, for the presence of alcoholic beverages.

I FULLY UNDERSTAND THAT THE CONDITIONS ON THIS PAGE HAVE THE SAME FORCE AND EFFECT AS THE STANDARD ORDER OF DISCRETIONARY PAROLE OR MANDATORY PAROLE AND ALL CONDITIONS LISTED ABOVE MUST BE FOLLOWED WHETHER I SIGN OR NOT.

Refused to Sign
Parolee   Witness

5/10/09
Dated   Title

FIG. 1D

Alaska Board of Parole
SUPPLEMENTAL CONDITIONS OF MANDATORY PAROLE

TANNER, Jerry L.   CASE#3PA-S07-00316CR.

33. **NO DRUG PARAPHERNALIA, NO DRUG POSSESSION, AND SUBMISSION TO DRUG TESTING / MONITORING / SEARCHES:** I will not at any time have on my person, in my residence or in my vehicle or any vehicle under my control any paraphernalia normally associated with the illicit use of drugs. This includes but is not limited to: syringes, injecting needles, cooking spoons, hash pipes, cocaine spoons, weighing scales and substances used for cutting, packaging or diluting drugs. I will submit to testing at any reasonable time upon request by or at the direction of a parole officer or peace officer to determine whether or not I have used any narcotic, stimulant, depressant, amphetamine, barbiturate, inhalant, or prescription drug. This testing includes but is not limited to blood test or urinalysis. I understand that if any of these tests show that I have ingested drugs not specifically prescribed by a licensed physician, my parole may be revoked. Refusing to cooperate when requested to submit to testing will constitute a violation of this condition and may result in revocation of my parole. Upon request by or at the direction of a parole officer or peace officer at any reasonable time, I will submit to a search of my person, my personal property, my residence, my vehicle or any vehicle under which I have control, for the presence of narcotic, hallucinogenic, stimulant, depressant, amphetamine, barbiturate or other drugs, or drug paraphernalia.

34. **SEARCH FOR WEAPONS:** Upon request by or at the direction of a parole officer at any reasonable time, I will submit to a search of my person, my personal property, my residence, my vehicle or any vehicle under my control, for the presence of deadly weapons as defined in AS 11.81.900(15).

35. **INFORM EMPLOYER OF CRIMINAL HISTORY:** I will advise any employer or prospective employer of my criminal history. I understand my parole officer may discuss the circumstances of my criminal history with my present employer or prospective employer.

36. **ADVISE P.O. OF MOTORIZED VEHICLE(S):** Before I drive a vehicle, I will provide information to my parole officer about any motorized vehicle that I own, lease, am buying or operate. I will advise my parole officer of the make, model, year, color and license number of the vehicle(s).

I FULLY UNDERSTAND THAT THE CONDITIONS ON THIS PAGE HAVE THE SAME FORCE AND EFFECT AS THE STANDARD ORDER OF DISCRETIONARY PAROLE OR MANDATORY PAROLE AND ALL CONDITIONS LISTED ABOVE MUST BE FOLLOWED WHETHER I SIGN OR NOT.

Refused to Sign
Parolee

5/18/09
Dated

Witness

Title

FIG. 1E

REFUSAL TO SIGN
MANDATORY PAROLE SUPERVISION TERMS/CONDITIONS

Alaska Board of Parole
550 West 7th Ave., Suite 601
Anchorage, AK 99501

Parolee Name: **Tanner, Jerry L.** (printed name) DOB: **7/27/61** OBSCIS #: **363693**

The Order of Mandatory Parole, including all general and supplemental conditions attached hereto were presented to **Tanner, Jerry L** (printed inmate name), at **Palmer Correctional Cntr** (place), on **5/18/09** (date), at **3:40 PM** (time). The prisoner was requested by the undersigned to read and sign them as evidence that the prisoner had read and understood them. The prisoner failed and refused to do so. The prisoner was given a copy of all conditions and advised that failure to strictly follow all conditions could result in the prisoner's arrest and serving all good time credited upon release.

Additional Information: _____

WITNESS: _____
(printed name of witness)

_____ **5/18/09**
(signature of witness) (date)

DISTRIBUTION: Original: Parole Board Office   cc: Prisoner File
                                                     Field Parole Officer
                                                     Prisoner

Rev. 1/99; Alaska Board of Parole [g:\parole\forms\Refusal to Sign MR.doc]

FIG. 1F. My Refusal to Sign

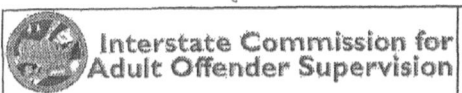

FIG. 2. My Application for Transfer to Ohio

CHAPTER 2
GOING THROUGH THE MOTIONS

The Monotony of Days

To some extent, my first days and months after my family went home became a succession of somewhat mindless, regular excursions to places that were familiar, and where a body might either fit in among all the other anonymous bodies wandering around, or be as invisible as all of the other invisible souls in the place—like Wal-Mart or Office Depot, for instance—or where customers intently gathered essential foodstuffs and such, paying little heed to anyone else but their screaming kids—like Carr's grocery market. I just tried not to make eye contact with anyone. I found I could go to the Alaska Club gym fairly regularly and feel relatively safe; the gym, after all, is a place that one goes where the focus in on oneself, on one's personal health and fitness (if you go there for the right reasons), and not so much on who else happens to be there working on their own personal health and fitness. My days, at least some of them, became a round-robin of visits to these innocuous, transparent places where the people were hardly distinguishable from the mannequins.

And yet, I seemed to have plenty of more important things to do. It felt like there was always a mound of paperwork from my attorneys that I had to sift through, documents I had to sign and then get in the car, drive out to Kinko's to make copies for my records, and then on to the Post Office to mail them back. I must have spent a fortune in postage alone. Most of the legal paperwork had to do with my epic and seemingly endless battle with Stoner, my former partner, over I-Care in Maine. That proceeding had turned into a virtual tennis match of legal motions and counter-motions, and every time my attorneys had to respond to any of them it would cost me $2,000 to $4,000 a pop. Yet, with constant postponements, new hearings, adjournments, and new motions, it seemed the case would drag on forever and never get resolved. More times than I care to remember, I found myself writing checks to my legal counsel to the tune of $15,000 to $20,000. It was draining me, financially and emotionally. Consequently, there were a lot of trips to the Post Office—and the bank— usually to the bank, *then* to the Post Office! For some reason, my attorneys didn't seem to mind that the case was taking so long.

Second only to that mountain of paperwork was the one associated with my status as a parolee and registered sex offender, in connection with which the state of Alaska Department of Corrections seemed intent on generating an endless stream of documents I had to sign and return, or regular filings and reports I had to make to remain in good standing with the parole board. I learned early on that, not only must I religiously make copies of these documents and filings for myself, for every item I mailed back to them, I had to send it certified return receipt requested (more postage expense!). As is so typical with government—both state and federal—I was the one held responsible for making sure executed documents got to where and to whom they were supposed to, on time. If a Post Office mailing delay meant that documents were delivered late, or worse, if some DOC bureaucrat lost one of my documents, it was my fault. So I did everything I could to be able to demonstrate that I had made a good-faith effort to stay on top of all of this and to be in compliance with the DOC's rules, regulations, and requirements. Bluntly stated, it was all a pain in the ass, and I couldn't help but think—and believe—that much of this was designed solely so that lots of state DOC employee bureaucrats could justify their existence. In any event, at home I was filling file cabinets with volumes of copies of documents that I fully expected no one would ever even read the original, but would probably stick in a different file cabinet in some office somewhere else.

Even this mundane routine of trips to the local stores, the gym, the bank and the post office felt risky. I was having tremendous difficulty just trusting other people. Most Sundays I would go to church, except when I was feeling especially down and vulnerable, and even with that, I was searching for a congregation where I might feel more comfortable, and more welcome; where I might be among people and hopefully under the guidance of a pastor who wouldn't judge me. At the end of each day it was often a great relief just to come home, close the door on the world, and be by myself. It was the only place I felt reasonably safe. I spent most evenings mindlessly watching television or movies, or on the computer writing or answering emails, or playing video games. It was such a colossal waste of time. So much did I want to feel safe and protected in my own space that I often turned down invitations from friends who wanted me to come over to their places for dinner, or to watch a ball game on TV. And there were many days where I slept in, or decided I just wasn't going to go out the door that day for anything. I did a lot of soul searching during the weeks and months that followed my release, but I can't say that the search revealed very much. I wasn't particularly proud of squandering my life this way, but sometimes it was all I could do to get through the day. I felt ashamed—yet, for no reason that I was responsible for—and I felt hurt in ways that nobody could really help me, and I pondered over and over the unfortunate sequence of events that had plunged me into this state of being. I yearned to go back to Ohio to be with my family again, yet I tried not to burden my parents too much with the way I was feeling. After all, there was nothing they could do to help from 4,000 miles away, and telling them about how I was feeling would only make them worry about me more. Besides, they both had enough troubles of their own. We did talk on the phone a lot, and that certainly helped to get through the rough days. Ultimately though, I felt like the shell of a human being going through the artificial motions of an existence, and it was not at all pleasant.

Old "Friends"

Barely a week after Uncle Roger left, somewhere around mid-August, I was surprised to get a phone call from Jim Lewis. Jim had been one of my fellow inmates at Palmer, and he called to tell me that he had been transferred from PCC to the jail in Anchorage because he needed to undergo some sort of foot surgery. Jim was a reasonably good guy—that is, when he was sober. When he was drunk, which on the outside seemed like most of the time, he was obnoxious and prone to be violent. Anyway, I talked on the phone with Jim for about 20 minutes or so, and wished him well on his surgery. As soon as I hung up, however I called PO Matthews to let him know that I had just had "contact"—and a conversation as well—with another convicted felon.

I did this, of course, because one of the conditions of my parole, number 11 on the hit parade, forbade me from having any contact whatsoever with prisoners or felons. The Order of Mandatory Parole specifically states: "I may not telephone, correspond with or visit any person confined in a prison, penitentiary, correctional institution or camp, jail, halfway house, work release center, community residential center, juvenile correctional center, etc." After reading that, I had to seriously ponder what could possibly be left that would be covered by the abbreviated "et cetera" at the end of the statement!

In direct contrast to this strict and unequivocal policy, PCC (and presumably also Anchorage jail, from which Jim Lewis had called me) had a pretty liberal policy regarding telephone use by inmates, even by the standards one might imagine for a minimum security facility. First there were quite a number of phones—and phone time—available. Each of Palmer's four wings on two floors had two telephones for inmate use, and the common area of the prison had a bank of eight phones for inmate use, all neatly numbered. And the phones were all turned on from 8:00 am to 9:00 pm. Of course, all inmate conversations were monitored and recorded. I certainly knew this. So, did I become paranoid when I got this call from Jim? You're damn straight I did. Because I also knew that those clever corrections officers had nailed any number of people for discussing things, or talking to people, that they weren't supposed to talk about, or to, and then hit them up with further violations, or citations of "bad behavior," and consequently, those offenders would receive more jail or parole time. Some of the more incorrigible people in there were, to put it bluntly, just too foolish, stupid, or oblivious to realize that if they discussed on the phone the next "caper" they had planned for when they got out, they instantly incriminated themselves and earned more time "in the joint" for their behavior violations.

(Then again, I suppose one would have to concede that they were no more stupid than today's politicians and teenagers who post idiotic, self-incriminating texts and videos on the internet.)

In hindsight, if the telephone policy at PCC seems unjustifiably liberal, one might speculate that the corrections department is pretty sly in using all that phone access as a crime-fighting tool—catching criminals in the planning stage before they ever have the opportunity to execute, or nailing parolees on the outside who were just up to no good, and should never have been released in the first place. Who else did the corrections officers think these guys were going to call—their mothers?

So I called Mr. Matthews right away. Naturally, I got his voice mail, so all I could do was leave him a recorded message telling him that Jim had called me from jail and we had had a conversation for a few minutes. Well, okay, the date was August 16th, and it was a Sunday, after all. Still, I was less than two months out of prison on parole and really, still walking on eggs, desperately fearful of doing anything wrong by way of a violation that would seriously piss off my "handlers" and send me back to prison. So I followed that voicemail message by getting on the computer and sending Mr. Matthews an email with the same information. I was always fearful of leaving messages that my PO or other people in authority over me could, true or not, deny ever receiving, and which of course I could not prove otherwise. I would not hear a peep from my PO for over a week, despite sending him several follow-up emails and worrying myself sick with the thought that I might have done something to get myself in trouble by talking to Jim Lewis, even though he was the one who called me. The fear and anxiety lurked in the back of my mind all of this time, and all I was trying to do was the right thing. In fact, I had heard nothing at all from Mr. Matthews since the meeting in late July when he told me that my transfer request to Ohio had been denied. It was one of his more disturbing habits to go on "radio silence" for long periods of time that were agonizing for me.

Then, on a Tuesday morning, some nine days later, I was having my morning coffee when PO Matthews accompanied by some unidentified woman showed up, unannounced of course, at my doorstep. They came into my apartment and snooped around brusquely, as parole officers do, I imagined. Then we sat down at my kitchen table, Mr. Matthews opened up his briefcase and pulled out a new set of parole documents for resubmitting my request for transfer to Ohio. He pointed out that Ohio would not, categorically, even consider the request if I continued to refuse to sign off on all of the conditions of parole, and he slid a new set of papers over to me for signature. Exasperated and frustrated, but determined and more resolved than ever to go home to be with my family, I rapidly signed everything that PO Matthews told me to sign, advice of counsel be damned. Once again my attorneys' advice—not to sign the papers in the first place—had resulted in no appreciable benefit or advantage to me or my situation, was in fact useless to me and utterly counterproductive to my effort to receive a sanctioned transfer to Ohio, and yet (of course) I had to pay for this flawed legal counsel which had availed me nothing.

In any event, as we were going over the paperwork, I happened to mention that the Alaska State Fair was coming up, and that I was planning to go with a group of friend. And, perhaps stupidly, I asked PO Matthews if that was okay. He replied flatly, "No. Not with your convictions." Then, more concerned about the phone call than ever, I asked, "Did you get my messages, you know, about talking to Jim Lewis on the phone a couple of weeks ago?"

"Hell," Matthews answered cavalierly, "I don't care about any of that. Talk to anybody you want."

Now, to be completely fair, the condition in the order of parole does allow one's parole officer to use his or her discretion with respect to contact with prisoners or felons. It states that "any knowing contact with a felon is prohibited unless approved by my PO," and further requires that, "I will notify my PO the next working day if I have contact with a prisoner or felon." But every time I mentioned such contacts, Matthews gave me the same curt response. "Don't care," he'd say, half the time not even looking up from the paperwork he was perpetually and intently scrutinizing whenever I had a meeting with him. This was a real concern to me, because it was about this time that I started hearing from or otherwise encountering some of my old "classmates" at PCC; some who had done their time and were released on society again (Jim Lewis would be released sometime in September, much to the delight of all the bars and liquor stores in Anchorage), some who were still in, and some who had done their time, been released, committed *another* offense (usually a violation of parole!), and had gone back in to do some more time on the taxpayer's dime. "Three hots and a cot," as inmates like to say. After a while, when Matthews seemed to be getting annoyed and exasperated at being asked the same question over and over (his response morphed from "Don't care," to "I don't give a shit!"), I just stopped asking. But of course, I could never be very comfortable about that. In fact, in one instance Matthews said, "If I find I have a problem with any of that, I'll let *you* know," emphasizing the word "you." So I knew that he must be getting reconnaissance from the good folks at PCC who were monitoring the inmates' calls. Again, not a situation that I could be very comfortable with at all, since I had no control over which reprobate might call me or what they wanted to talk about!

I will say that between this refreshingly non-suspicious attitude and his willingness to help me with resubmitting my transfer paperwork so that it would pass muster in two states, what I was learning was that, as parole officers go (in my limited experience) Greg Matthews seemed to be a pretty regular and reasonable guy. He was clearly very experienced at what he did, he didn't seem to be genetically programmed to be suspicious that I was going to automatically go out and do bad things or try to get away with stuff—I bet he could probably spot a faker or conniver in an instant—and he appeared to be one PO who focused on the really important things, willing to let the small innocuous stuff slide. I'd even venture to say that Matthews would try to keep his charges out of serious trouble if he could, which, to my way of thinking, is about all that one could reasonably ask of one's parole officer. I should have considered myself lucky: It would be a completely different story when I finally made it to Ohio.

And yet, what did all that matter? So PO Matthews turned out to be a somewhat reasonably good guy. So what? If he had been a prick, he could have used any of those contacts to immediately cite me for being in violation of parole. If he had been a "good guy" for 364 days a year and decided, just for the hell of it, to be a prick for one day, he could, with the scribble of his signature on some DOC violation form or other, revoke my parole on the spot and consign me back to prison. I would have no recourse to a hearing or to presenting my side of the story. When you are on parole, I learned, you simply have no rights, and you are completely at the mercy of the state. Or, as a parole officer might put it, you have *no rights except those* the parole board and your individual parole officer decide that you may have—and they can actually take them back any time they feel like it!

Discretion is a wonderful concept, but in some respects, discretion might encourage or allow a person to do something they truly believe is sanctioned, only to be hit over the head with it later on. To state it differently, discretion in this context allows an authority regime to arbitrarily, and without due process, decide that an individual has violated its regulations or requirements of conduct, and to punish that individual without appeal. The goal, it would seem, is to keep you guessing, to keep you scared. Many—and I would argue most—of the so-called conditions of parole are like this, and virtually any one of them can be used—twisted, I would argue—to construe a trumped-up charge of violation of parole, against which there is no mechanism of legal defense or appeal process. That is why my legal counsel so strongly advised me against signing off on the parole conditions in the first place.

To this day I wonder: I'd be willing to bet that if I hadn't mentioned the state fair and asked Matthews's permission to go, if I'd simply gone with my friends and had a good time, even if it came to his attention at some point later on, I'll bet he wouldn't have said "Boo" about it afterwards. In fact, I'll bet he might have even said it was okay for me to go if that unidentified woman wasn't there when I asked. When you're in law enforcement, you know, you've got to look tough and authoritative and make the hard decisions, dontcha?

Actually, it was not very long after I was released that I suddenly began to learn just how many people I had apparently made friends with during my 16-month sojourn in PCC—both among the inmates and the working staff of corrections and support at the facility. Because, unbeknownst to my less-than-vigilant PO, I had been carrying on with regular email correspondence with a number of "pen-pal" inmates at Palmer since I got out. (I owned up to this that same morning when Matthews and his girlfriend showed up at my place and I finally had the chance to tell him, face to face, about Jim Lewis's call, but he didn't care about the email contacts either!) And not long after I got that phone call from Jim Lewis, I started getting calls and letters and emails from all sorts of people, and some days it seemed like my phone would ring off the hook. Some of them were from really bad guys—the ones who really deserved to be in Palmer, or honestly, someplace even worse, as far as I was concerned. I got rid of them right away, or tried to, by telling them if they called me again I'd report them to my PO. Some of them called multiple times regardless of this threat. That's when, knowing that the calls were monitored and recorded, I was the most nervous, and wanted to make it clear that not only was I not a willing party to this conversation, I was trying to put a stop to these people calling me ever again. It seemed to me that they could be used against me regardless of my intentions.

Mostly, the worst of them were, quite outrageously, calling to ask me for money! I guess you can't keep any secrets in jail. Everybody in there undoubtedly knew from the press reports in the papers that I had once run a couple of multi-million dollar companies, and naturally they presumed that I was still wealthy—perhaps they thought I had mattresses stuffed with neat packs of hundred dollar bills. It's wryly amusing to me now, but if they only knew how the courts and my own attorneys in three states were bleeding me dry, they wouldn't have bothered to waste their dime to make the call!

And yet on the other hand, there were a number of people whom I thought were really decent guys who had simply made some really bad choices in their lives. One of them was Darren, a 22- or 23-year-old kid who was in PCC for grand theft auto at the same time that I was there, and whom I had tried to help with encouragement by stressing that he was still young and could turn his life around if he put his mind to it. Without trivializing it, Darren's story could be summed up pretty simply: he got in with the wrong crowd, got messed up with drugs and alcohol (like so many other people in Palmer), and was riding in a stolen car with his buddies when it was involved in a crash in which someone was killed. He was lucky that he was convicted only of auto theft, and not manslaughter. Unfortunately, I learned that Darren had joined that third category of inmates that I mentioned earlier—the ones who did their time, got released, did more crimes, and went back in. I was really sad to hear about this. I had hoped that Darren would make a new life for himself when he got out. Instead, with a few months of being released on parole, Darren rejoined his buddies and got caught in another carjacking and went back into PCC. They might just as well as kept his old bunk warm for him.

I must have gotten emails, letters and phone calls from a dozen or more of my former colleagues in PCC, and I always felt obliged to write back or respond in some way. Having met them, talked to them, and gotten to know them, I believed they were mostly good guys, which I still believe today, for the most part. But I also knew that most of them had little or no support on the outside, and in some cases their families had abandoned them. I thought it was the least I could do to talk or correspond with them to lend what little support I could offer.

I also kept in touch with several friends among the staff that worked at PCC, particularly Janet, who lived in Eagle River and was my boss when I worked in the shipping department for the prison. She had started working for the Department of Corrections at the Anchorage Jail until taking the job as shipping manager for PCC. For all I have to say in this book that might seem negative about the bureaucracy of the DOC or about the inconsistent and often counter-productive aspects of the parole system and the people who run it, I want to acknowledge that there were some pretty good, genuine people who cared and tried to do the right thing. After all, the name of the department is "corrections," which ought to imply that people who have made mistakes nevertheless have the capacity to "correct" their behavior. It is not, for example, the "Department of Incarceration."

In any case, from the first day I went to work in Palmer's shipping department during my incarceration there (earning every penny of my inmate salary of 60 cents an hour!), Janet said to me, "If you respect me, I'll respect you," and we quickly became good friends; we still keep in touch even today. Whenever Janet came to Anchorage, she'd give me a call and we'd go out for coffee or lunch. She was checking up on me—making sure I was doing okay and getting readjusted to life "on the outside," and I like to think of Janet as a "diamond in the rough." What I mean by that is she was a unionized state employee with 30 years of experience working in the rough and tumble environment of a correctional system populated by some pretty miserable and ornery characters—not to mention the inmates—and yet she had a truly good heart, she tried to see the good in people, and she certainly gave me the benefit of the doubt. Janet was bold enough, when for example she perceived a particular situation to be unfair, to stand up and say, "This isn't right," even to go to the point of confronting her superiors to tell them what she thought about it, and perhaps effect some positive change. In Palmer, we had worked seamlessly together, just like any other workplace out in the public sector. Now that I was out of there and struggling a bit, I could always count on some positive support from Janet when I was feeling down about my predicament.

In fact, I was friends with other state workers from the corrections department, including, remarkably enough, some of the guards, though none so pure as Janet. One of them was Meg Burton, who was the Secretary to the Sergeant at PCC. Meg was a nice person at heart, divorced, who had apparently made a few bad choices of her own, which may have been the reason that she always seemed to have money troubles, despite having a moderately well-paying full time job as a unit secretary with the state. After meeting and doing some work with her in PCC (since of course my shipping department duties entailed significant interaction with the administration of the facility), I had remained friends with Meg after I was released. Then one day she called and told me her dogs were sick and needed medical attention, but she didn't have the money to pay the veterinarian. She asked me if she could borrow $500 to pay the vet, and promised to pay it back as soon as she could. I couldn't help but see the bitter irony of a state DOC worker asking a former inmate for a loan. Although, I would later come to the rather disheartening realization that Meg was a bit of an operator, and smart enough to recognize a soft touch when she met one. I mean, who could say 'no' to helping a couple of sick dogs for a friend? So I called the vet myself and gave him my credit card number to pay the bill, which of course, she promised to repay as soon as she could.

Well, after that I was something of a marked man for Meg, and a short time later, when she was having vehicle problems, she asked me if she could borrow a Dodge Durango I owned but used infrequently. Soft touch or not, by that point I could see the writing on the wall, and I politely said, "I'm sorry, but no." Even later, when I decided to sell the Durango, Meg expressed an interest in buying it, even though both she and I knew that she was hopelessly unable to afford it, and I wondered if she expected me to help her finance it. "Meg," I said as gently as I could, "You'll just have to go to the bank and get a car loan like anybody else." Not surprisingly, I soon lost touch with Meg, although I later learned that she was terminated with cause from her job at PCC, so I can only assume that things did not get any easier for her. Of course, once she was fired, I knew I wasn't going to ever get back the $500 I had loaned her to take care of her dogs!

You may be wondering why I have gone on at length here to describe the friendly relationships and interactions I had with inmates and former inmates, and with some of the regular working staff of the DOC that continued even after I got out of PCC. To begin with, I think the reason that I began to get phone calls and letters from so many of the inmates was that I was always someone who would listen to their stories and their talk about their problems without judging them, and with a kind of empathy that no one else would give them. More importantly, I know that I had earned the trust and respect of the state workers that I stayed friends with after my release, and that was terribly important for me; for my self-esteem, and for the idea that I was not the kind of monster that my "criminal" record might suggest to some people. But even more critically, that hurtful portrayal was eclipsed by this highly restrictive list of "conditions" of parole, which themselves suggested that I was capable of even more heinous behavior, from drug use to distribution to pedophilia, things that I regard as simply abhorrent, and wanted—somehow, some way—to prove I was never capable of doing. How do you prove that something doesn't exist?

However, it took me several months to realize that these calls and letters from the guys still inside were dragging me down. At first, it all felt like a great deal of support coming my way, and even if they persisted in telling me about their own ongoing and seemingly endless problems, I was desperate for any kind of support I could get. In a sense, the guys inside were "friendly" voices; people who had no authority over me, who could not tell me what to do or how high to jump (like the parole board), but were instead people I could talk with and commiserate with, one on one. Still, I began to realize that in many ways they were latching onto me for their own selfish support rather than the other way around. There was a kind of imbalance here, and I was expending a tremendous amount of personal energy playing psychologist and psychotherapist, I was squandering a tremendous amount of emotional capital in analyzing and pondering their troubles and their issues, and it was seriously draining me, both emotionally and physically. I certainly couldn't solve everybody's problems, and the especially bedeviling thing was when despite my advice or words of encouragement, some of these guys went right out and did the exact same things that got them into trouble in the first place, like Darren had done. I was often left scratching my head, because I just couldn't understand for the life of me how some of these guys think, or where on earth they came up with some of the illogical and irrational things they believed to be true, and hatched the hare-brained stunts they pulled that eventually sent them to prison as repeat offenders. It was utterly baffling, and eventually the number of calls and letters began to drive me fairly crazy.

But it wasn't just the number of calls. It was that talking with these guys could also be pretty exasperating. I could pour my own heart out trying to support these guys, listen ad nauseam to their often tragic stories, and offer my best positive thoughts and whatever wisdom I could muster by way of advice, and they would turn around and totally ignore it anyway, just the way Darren had done. It was often all for nothing as far as doing any good for them, and as I said earlier, for me, a colossal waste of emotional and psychological energy such that, after a while, I had to ask myself, "Why the hell am I wasting my time with all of this?" I realized that many of them were in fact just leaning on me or outright using me (this was fairly easy to recognize in the ones who simply wanted to "borrow" some money), and it was sucking the very life force out of me. More than once I actually wrote in my journal that I had to "stop helping people all the time." Which, for me, was a terrible thing to actually say; something that goes against my very nature. Helping other people in this life is what I believe in most of all. I had spent the better part of my lifetime helping thousands of people through my healthcare companies, and the idea of having to shut out people who were in need was abhorrent to me. However, the fact of the matter was that I needed to concentrate on my own situation. I needed to get on with my life. That meant, actually, I needed to *"get a life,"* in the first place, since at this time I really felt like I didn't have one, and it wasn't going to be an easy thing to do.

CHAPTER 3
A JAIL WITHOUT BARS

Anchored Down

It was never the case that I tried to deliberately or provocatively "test" the limits of my ostensible freedom under parole—what in jailhouse jargon is called "being on paper"—rather, and quite to the contrary, it was simply that I tried to live as normal a life as I could under the circumstances. After all, I had done my time. Okay, being that I was still "on paper" I was actually still finishing up my time. So be it. My view of parole was that it ought to be a time during which I should have the opportunity to demonstrate through my deeds and actions that I wanted to return to living a productive life, that I wanted to get back into some kind of worthwhile work, and that I wanted to be a contributing member of society again.

There were a number of performance requirements that I was more or less fully informed of, and with which I was obliged to comply with—to the letter—both as a registered sex offender and as a matter of keeping in good standing as a parolee, parole being in some respects an extension of the state DOC's jurisdiction, outside the prison walls, over my daily activities, travel, and my "behavior" in general. I'll call these my "known knowns," to borrow Donald Rumsfeld's peculiar (and yet acrobatically profound and illustrative) terminology.

For example, as a registered sex offender (it still rankles me, and it still cuts painfully into my soul, to have to call myself that) I was required to report to the local state trooper's barracks every three months without fail. There I was required to fill out a long form with all of my personal information—current address, phone numbers and email addresses, the make, model, and license plate numbers of all vehicles I might be driving, and so on; virtually all of the vital statistics of my existence at that moment. Failure to comply with this requirement would result in the issuance of an immediate warrant for my arrest, as well as represent a violation of my parole.

I could understand and accept this. What I thought absurd about it was that I had to fill out this form all over again each time I reported in even if none of this information had changed since the last report three months ago. It felt a lot like being forced by one's elementary school teacher to write, "I will not disrupt the class" 50 times on the blackboard every three months.

In addition, as a parolee, I was required to meet periodically, though on a somewhat irregular basis, with my Parole Officer. The "irregular basis" of those meetings was essentially at Officer Matthews's discretion or whim; call it what you will. If he called me for a meeting, I had to make damn sure to get there, and I had to set aside any other plans or obligations I might have had for that day or time. Finally, I could be called at any time to report to the barracks to take a polygraph test, often on very short notice. If I failed for any reason to comply with any of these strict requirements, I would be deemed to be in violation of parole, and as a consequence, likely to have my parole revoked and be returned to PCC to do the remainder of my sentence. Officer Matthews and a number of the other DOC authorities liked to refer to parolees' full compliance with all of these reporting requirements a matter of "mutual respect," but they should have left the word "mutual" out, because there was nothing "mutual" about it—it was instead a decidedly one-way affair of homage to authority.

For one thing, if I was called to a meeting with my PO or to come to take yet another polygraph, I was expected to drop everything, no matter how personally important it was, and report as ordered. Here again, I might have expected that—I am the "criminal," in this equation, after all. But if circumstances were such that it was going to be simply—and legitimately—impossible for me to make it to a meeting, when I called in to try to arrange a postponement, I had to speak directly to Officer Matthews, or one of the other POs if Matthews was unavailable. I was not allowed to leave a voicemail message or send an email; those didn't count, and failure to speak directly to a PO would represent—you guessed it—a violation of parole. There was one occasion that this happened which further serves to illustrate how cavalier and flippant the parole office, and PO Matthews in particular, were with regard to scheduling these meetings on a whim. In early October of 2009, I looked at the calendar and suddenly realized that Officer Matthews had set up a meeting for the 19th, which happened to be the date that Alaska Day was to be observed that year. Alaska Day commemorates the formal transfer of the Territory of Alaska from Russia to the United States, and it's a legal holiday there, meaning that all state offices—including those of the parole board—are closed! So it was up to me to make the phone calls, to point out the error to my PO and set up a new date for us to meet.

Conversely, Officer Matthews was quite clearly under no legal obligation to advise me whenever he had to cancel one of our scheduled meetings. Nor apparently did he seem to feel any moral or ethical obligation to do so, because there were a number of instances when I would show up at his office for a meeting as duly ordered, only to learn from the secretary that Matthews was not there or was out of the office for the day, on what might have been "official" business, but could just as easily have been personal pursuits like, say, fishing. Never mind "moral or ethical obligation," how about letting me know just as a matter of human decency? So much for the notion of "mutual" respect. That, I quickly learned, was a crock of shit. And of course, whenever this occurred, it was *my* responsibility to contact my PO to reschedule our appointment—Matthews would never contact me in order to do that.

The same could be said for the random lie detector tests, which I felt were an absolute joke. I passed every one of them, which pleased Officer Matthews certainly, but it was frustrating to me because, as I implored to him many times, "Why would I lie to you?" I said to Matthews over and over, "I've got nothing to hide; my life is an open book." I saw no useful purpose for these humiliating and time consuming polygraphs that effectively wasted an entire day each time I was required to take one. Yet, there would be more of them as long as I was on paper. And, if whatever reason the authorities wanted to bust me back to the hallowed halls of PCC, all they would have had to do was determine that I had lied on the test, and would have been as good as drawing a "Go Directly to Jail" card in the Monopoly game that is the world of the DOC in Alaska, and, I suspect, probably in every DOC in every state in America.

This was all fine: at least I knew and understood that this was going to be the way things were while I was on parole. These were, as I said earlier, the "known knowns" of my new reality. I could have felt sorry for myself, and I confess that I often did. But I also firmly resolved to adopt an existential perspective much like that of Camus in that I would do everything I could to build a relatively normal life amid decidedly abnormal circumstances. I would adapt to these new circumstances. I would try to build a new business in one field or another, I would try to tell my story in memoir form in a published book, I would try to enjoy the life I still had with my family and friends, and I would endeavor with determination to move forward with my life. And this is where I encountered the whole host of "unknown unknowns" that would severely impact my ability to pursue all of those worthwhile goals, and even go so far as to prevent me from being able to go after them, much less actually achieve them.

Nothing but Roadblocks

How naïve was I about what being on parole and a registered sex offender really means! My understanding, under the terms of my release, was that I would be permitted to travel on a limited basis as long as I reported and registered my travel plans with my PO and received the parole board's express permission. In October, I informed Officer Matthews that I was planning a pleasure trip to Las Vegas to meet up with my Uncle and some other friends and family for a long weekend, the 19th through the 21st of November, right before Thanksgiving. I also planned to take a trip to Ohio to be with my family over the Christmas and New Year's holidays, from December 14th through January 8th, 2010. Both routine, family oriented excursions, not even any business dealings planned, just the way millions of Americans travel every year to be with their families over those precious holidays.

Officer Matthews seemed fine with it; at least, he expressed no misgivings about it, or gave any indication that there might be a problem with this request, leaving me with the impression that this was a pretty routine thing, and nothing to be concerned about. And indeed, why should it be otherwise? However, he did inform me that I needed to purchase my airline tickets and to give him copies or documentation of their purchase, because, as he said rather matter-of-factly, the parole board would need to see them in order to confirm my exact travel plans and itineraries before they would approve my proposed trips. That seemed reasonable to me, so I went out and bought my tickets somewhere around October 20th, and gave Officer Matthews copies of the documentation he needed. Being instructed to actually go ahead and buy the—as everyone knows, *non-refundable*—airline tickets only served to further bolster my belief that there was nothing unusual or problematic about my requests for permission to travel out of state. And I waited for approval confirmation from the board. I assumed it would not take long, since the Vegas trip was only a month away. And I waited.

A week went by with no response. Then another. No word. I began to get that sinking feeling that I had grossly overestimated the chances that this thing was going to happen, or that it was all as routine as I had imagined it to be. Periodically I called or sent an email to Officer Matthews to inquire about the status of my request, but neither did he have any further word on it. Until my meeting with him on November 17th, two days before I was scheduled to leave for Las Vegas, when he finally told me that permission for both trips had been denied. Denied, even though I had done as I was instructed and gone out and bought the tickets for the pleasure of the parole board. And I realized in an instant that any attempt to travel beyond the borders of the State of Alaska—or more precisely, beyond the borders of the borough (county) of Alaska to which I was restricted—while "on paper" would be utterly futile. And costly, since I would have to buy my useless tickets in advance!

I remember reading somewhere that in the days leading up to the Civil War, Sam Houston implored his fellow Texans not to secede from the Union by saying, "Texas is too small to be a country, and too big to be an insane asylum." After my November 17th meeting with Officer Matthews, I realized that the Matanuska-Susitna Borough of Alaska would be my personal enormous asylum indefinitely, until such time as I was able to convince the parole board to let me go home to Ohio.

From the moment I was released from prison I was determined to start a new business; in fact, while I was still in Palmer I had instructed my attorneys to research some opportunities for me. I figured that while they were bleeding me dry in my legal fight with my former partner they might as well do something useful and constructive. The healthcare industry that I knew and loved was no longer an option; as a convicted felon I could no longer be a party to the types of state Medicare and Medicaid contracts involved in offering broad-based healthcare to the general public. However, the idea of acquiring a franchise really appealed to me. As I mentioned earlier, buying into an established franchise seemed like a terrific way of jump-starting a new business venture that I could make profitable in the space of a year or less. And one of the franchise opportunities I zeroed in on was Quiznos Restaurants, which specializes in toasted subs and sandwiches.

So I obtained the package of application instructions from Quiznos, all 2,500 pages and two and a half inches thick, and I filled out all of the forms with the required information. I wanted to do it up big-time: my proposal was to open not one location, but rather, three locations six months apart. I created a thorough, meticulous business plan that detailed how I planned to open one shop and work to get a staff hired and brought up to speed before opening the second restaurant, and so on. In this way I could bring some trained staff members to run the new locations to ensure that they would be run properly and efficiently right from the get-go. My plan was to begin building the franchise locations in Ohio immediately after I was transferred there. Most importantly of course, my business plan demonstrated how I would ensure the building of crucial positive cash flow throughout the rollout of the three locations. If I may say so myself, it was a brilliant, pinpoint business plan that took into account the most critical components required for any business to be successful and profitable. I spent hour upon hour preparing the paperwork, crossing every "t" and dotting every "i," and I submitted my application to the Quiznos organization in early September, less than three months after I was released from PCC. Naturally, of course, I was required to provide copies of all of this to my handlers at the DOC.

The parole board, flatly and unequivocally, said, "No."

And I heard for the first time a phrase that I would from then on hear repeatedly, such that it might easily have been the mantra of both the parole board and PO Matthews: "Not until you are 'off paper'." That is, to be clear, not until I was no longer "on parole." It was also the juncture, so early on after my release, that I began to wonder just what the hell was the point of my being out of prison "on parole" if I was going to be prohibited from doing anything to create a new and productive life for myself, or, as law enforcement people are also so fond of saying, to "turn my life around." The fact is, I would have liked to point out, I was doing just fine before all of this happened to me—I certainly didn't need any life-turning when I was providing competent and reliable healthcare services to thousands of people across two states. But that was it. Once the parole board spoke, the order was given, and there was no recourse; theirs was the final word. I had done a tremendous amount of work to file the application and create an airtight business plan, and it was all for naught. It would be pointless, it seemed, to look at any other business opportunities because it was emphatically clear that the parole board would refuse to approve those as well.

One thing the DOC couldn't prevent me from doing was writing my memoir, and at various times I buried myself in both writing it and negotiating with publishers and literary agents in the effort to have the book published as soon as it was completed. As with everything I do, I mounted a full scale assault toward making this happen. For instance, on one day alone—December 16, 2009—I sent out query letters to 43 book agents. I don't do anything half-assed. However, writing the book itself proved to be an arduous, intensive process that would take another two years (and two editors) to complete, and while I would doggedly see that process through to the end, I continued to try to find something productive that I could do for myself now, at the moment, trapped in my virtual jail.

But by far the very worst part of this very strict restraint on my activities and my movements is what it did to my personal relationships with my family and friends. When my Aunt Emma Jean passed away that August, I couldn't travel to attend the funeral. I had many sleepless nights largely because of that. When my dad had some serious health problems, which were starting to become more frequent at about this time, I couldn't go to Ohio to be with him and to help my mother cope with the situation. And when Jane Battier called in late October to tell me that her mother's health had taken a turn for the worse, where it not for my situation, I would have been on a plane to Maine the next day to be with and to support her. Jane had been my first manager of the Irish Setter Pub in Presque Isle, and a dear friend from the first day I met her. Throughout all of my difficulties—the personal ones with Russell Stoner and the legal ones in district court—and the whole time that I sat idly wasting my days in PCC, she had been my most loyal and compassionate supporter; as loyal and compassionate as my own parents. The dozens of letters that she wrote to me while I was in jail uplifted me and gave me hope that there would be better days ahead, when all of this was over. I have kept those letters to this day.

But when Jane's husband Jack called me on October 26th to tell me that Jane's mom had succumbed to the cancer, all I could do was send a damn card of condolence. Another funeral I could not attend and, in my mind, another profoundly personal obligation I could not meet. I felt as though I could not return the same compassion and concern, nor give the same support, that Jane had shown me all of the past several years.

So there I sat, stuck in Alaska, with my hands tied behind my back, figuratively speaking. I wasn't allowed to do anything, I wasn't allowed to go anywhere. Is it any wonder that I continued to fight severe depression and to experience constant anxiety with bouts of paranoia? My existence was ruled by the DOC, and they basically said, "You don't do anything unless we say it's okay first." On the successive monthly anniversaries of my release from prison—every 28th of the month—I found myself writing the same thing in journal: I was "free on parole" for "x" number of months but it still felt as though I was still inside the walls of PCC. For all practical purposes, I was "still in prison, it was just a bigger cell," I wrote in my journal. Virtually nothing had changed other than my geophysical position on the globe! It was taking a toll on my physical health. I was periodically experiencing blood in my urine as well as other inexplicable physical symptoms. I went to see my doctor, who asked me if I felt as though I was under a lot of stress.

"You think?" I shot back. Some typical entries from my journal during this time, toward the end of 2009, reveal a common theme:

> I just want to be alone and away from everyone! I am doing a lot of thinking about my life.... I am still very scared about a lot of things and I can't seem to feel that I can trust *anyone* at all! (August 23, 2009)
>
> Today is three months I have been out of jail but I feel as though I am still in; my life has not really changed and nothing has gotten any better. I feel that I am on the outside looking in. (September 28, 2009)
>
> I feel so lost! I am thinking too much and the thoughts are racing through my head. I am getting worried about what I am going to do. I feel so alone and I am feeling blue, but I am not letting anyone know how I feel (what good would it do anyway?), but I am keeping it all bottled up inside of me and that is killing me. I feel like I am going to lose everything I have worked so hard for over the past 11 years. At my age, how do you start over? (October 29, 2009)
>
> I feel down today, and not strong enough. I am trying to push myself to do things out of the house, but I am afraid and I really don't want to leave my safe place; because there is nothing for me out there anymore and I cannot trust anyone! I have no life at all! (November 4, 2009)
>
> I have been feeling blue lately and I think it is all the pressure that is on me from my

attorneys—attorneys in Alaska, attorneys in Maine, attorneys in Ohio ... and the state, and the DOC ... and just dealing with life. I feel like I am backed into a corner with no escape. Will it ever end? Plus I am having some problems with my thinking and with my memory. I think it is all coming down on my nerves! (November 20, 2009)

Throughout all of this time, of course, my application for transfer home was in irretrievable limbo. Whenever I asked Officer Matthews what the status of that request was, he would tell me that the parole board had heard nothing from the state of Ohio. Whenever my parents or attorneys would make similar inquiries with the appropriate authorities there, the Ohio DOC would tell them that they had not heard anything from the state of Alaska. This went on, month after month, and it was frustrating, and depressing as hell.

So it was that Christmas of 2009 was at best a pretty melancholy affair. I did not go out. I cooked a ham dinner for myself, as if the preparation of such a time-honored traditional meal might ease the pain of my isolation. It did not. I did get a lot of phone calls from my parents and friends, wishing me a Merry Christmas, and I them, and that helped a bit. But I stayed in on Christmas Day and for several days thereafter, not even going to church on Christmas Day, which fell on a Friday, or the following Sunday two days later. My journal entry for December 26th reads in part: "I wish God would take me home and I am ready to go." Now that I look back on it, I'm not sure which "home" I was referring to.

CHAPTER 4
DELIVERANCE DELAYED

Bureaucratic Bullshit

Christmas of 2009 was probably one of the lowest moments in my adult life. Being alone during a season that I had, for 50 years, intensely looked forward to and always had been able to spend with family and friends only served to underscore my isolation and exacerbate my despair and anxiety. The Christmas holidays are times that I deeply cherish and would not, willingly, miss for the world, and here, for the first time in my life, I was missing them; that is, I was missing what is most important about them, my family. Alaska, which had been an exciting, exhilarating place when I arrived 20 years earlier, and which had been very good to me in love and in business, now seemed more like the harsh, desolate and hostile place that I might have imagined it as a child, long before I ever had the notion to actually live and prosper here. Now all I wanted to do was leave it for good.

I was ready to just give up; never before in my life had I ever experienced such despair and loathing for my existence. December

28th marked six months out of prison, yet in my mind it had been six desperate months of house arrest with no clear end in sight—I was like a butterfly pinned to a plaque, except that I was still alive. In my journal for that date I wrote that, in reality, I had "no life at all." I was exhausted from being and feeling totally alone and kept away from my family, and worst of all, this was when I began to fear that I had no fight left in me. I was under the complete control of the state, the DOC, the parole board—whatever—all I knew was that I had absolutely no control over my own life. I had no control over anything—not the lawsuit with my former business partner and lover, not the prodigious amount of money that suit was costing me in legal fees, not the transfer application to Ohio, nor any of the incipit, deceitful games that the DOC and parole board kept playing—nothing. More than ever before, as Christmas Day approached and then after it receded, I shunned people, places and things, and I holed up in my apartment. I often didn't answer the phone; I just did not feel like talking to anyone. I felt old, and tired, and useless. At times I didn't even want to talk to my mom and dad because they could see right through me when I tried to put up a front by telling them I was "doing just fine." They knew it was a lie; that I was hurting, and I wanted to at least try to spare them that pain. I didn't dare go out unless I absolutely had to. For some time now I was no longer going to the Alaska Club gym, and in hindsight, I realize now that my physical well-being and my once positive psychological outlook were both suffering and getting worse as a result. In my journal I wrote that I did not know how much more of this untenable and intolerable situation I could take; many of my daily entries over these terrible days end with the same words: "Just another day in my prison." This malaise continued past New Year's Day and into January and threatened to utterly consume me. On January 6th, 2010 I wrote, "I think I am losing it." I felt like that very often, time and again.

1,825 DAYS OF HELL: ONE MAN'S ODYSSEY THROUGH THE AMERICAN PAROLE SYSTEM

What happened next is packed with a bunch of ironies. To begin with, I might have come to the point of never leaving my home again were it not for the fact that I had been ordered to appear at a parole meeting on January 12th. I was still very fearful of doing anything to upset the parole board or make them angry at me, or even to inadvertently commit a "violation"—Oh my! Which is ironic in and of itself, because the way I was feeling at this point, my utter despair and lack of any sense of self-worth was such that I might easily have thought, who cares? What else could they possibly do to me? After all, physical torture had probably been outlawed some years ago, even in Alaska! At this low point, if I committed some sort of violation of parole, or if I simply failed to perform some petty requirement that would put me in violation, the worst that would have happened was that they'd send me back to PCC to finish my time in jail. How would that be worse than this zombie existence I was leading as a citizen without rights with on the "outside"?

But, of course, I'm a person who plays by the rules, and I'm not a troublemaker. I was under the strict supervision of the state, and I would do as I was told. Plus, there was added importance to this particular appointment; I had been summoned to this meeting primarily to meet my new Parole Officer. Officer Matthews had been rather abruptly reassigned to another department; no other explanation was ever given for this, nor did I expect to be given one; the DOC never gave reasons, they simply gave orders. I did not sleep well at all the night before the day of the meeting, and I was up at 4:30 in the morning, drinking coffee and trying to stay calm. Fittingly, and oh so characteristically, when I got to the meeting at the parole office, the new Parole Officer I was supposed to meet *wasn't there*! Instead, I sat down with a female officer, whose name I do not recall, and she told me that my new parole officer was a Mr. Zsoly Nagyetevi. Then she hit me with the bombshell.

"Officer Matthews," she said, "Never filed your paperwork for your transfer application to Ohio."

I was dumbstruck. Six months I had waited and yearned anxiously for word about the only thing that I was truly certain that I wanted once I was released from prison—permission to go home to be with my family—and here absolutely nothing had done by DOC officials whose job it was, at least in part, to enable this to happen, and to carry out my request through proper channels. I did not know if this issue had anything to do with Officer Matthews's unexplained transfer, but the fact is, I sincerely doubted that. I had long since come to realize that the DOC didn't give a damn about me or about my welfare, or anything that might happen to me. They had shown absolutely no concern for my situation whatsoever, and it would be utterly ridiculous, even laughable, to even imagine that they would actually punish or discipline one of their own for failing to do his job in terms of taking care of a felon "in the system." To them I was just another number, #363963, and just one more cog in the machinery of the correctional system in these United States. To add insult to injury, since my new PO, Mr. Nagyetevi, had failed to show up for this initial meeting on January 4th, I would have to *wait until my next parole meeting* to start the process of filing for permission to transfer all over again! That meeting was scheduled for February 3rd, and I was also supposed to take a polygraph examination at this meeting. I could only hope and pray that Officer Nagyetevi would actually show up for this one—you would think that he would want to be there to observe my lie detector test. And just to cap things off, the woman parole officer who told me all of this also informed me that the process would likely take up to 90 days, not the 45 days that Officer Matthews had originally indicated. Thus, to my mind, I faced at least four more months of house arrest—and that was if everything went off without a hitch, something the DOC had heretofore never managed to accomplish.

And yet, in a bizarre way, all of this depressing and infuriating news gave me new hope. At least now I knew why—for over six months—nothing was happening with my transfer application, why there was no news at all. I now knew why Ohio wasn't hearing anything from Alaska—because they weren't!—and I also knew now why Alaska, in the guise of PO Matthews, wasn't hearing anything from Ohio—because he was lying about everything to begin with and Ohio had no I idea that I had even requested a transfer there! Hope is a curious, irrational phenomenon. While I had no reason whatsoever to expect my new PO to be any more competent or more responsible than Officer Matthews, I could hope that he might actually want to make up for this further injustice that had been done to me through Matthews's failure to do his job. Hell, I could even hope that he would actually file the paperwork like he was supposed to! And eventually he did, but he would take his sweet-assed time about it.

Because PO Nagyetevi once again failed to show up for our next meeting on February 3rd. When I duly arrived at the parole offices, first they told me that the polygraph examination that I was scheduled to take had already been postponed until February 17th ; no reason, no explanation, just postponed. "Come back then," they said. Then they informed me that Officer Nagyetevi had to cancel our meeting, and that my "next" meeting with him (it would still, in actuality, be our "first meeting"—if he actually showed up, that is) would be on March 4th. So, as happened so many times during my parole, I had wasted an entire day in going to the parole office for a meeting or a procedure that had been cancelled without my knowledge, or which no one from the

DOC had even the slightest courtesy to pick up the phone to call me and let me know of the cancelation. And there was nothing I could do but go home to wait some more.

On the 17th I was again at the parole office as duly ordered, where I submitted to the required polygraph examination. I watched all the little lights flicker, the pen gauges jump and twitter like seismograph readings while I wondered why my PO couldn't have dragged himself to the office to meet with me on that day, since I had to be there for the exam anyway. I passed the exam, as usual, and then I went home to wait once again for the next meeting with Officer Nagyetevi on March 4th. He actually showed up, and at last, we filled out the application forms one last time, and my transfer request was officially filed. Or so I hoped it would be this time.

Life Goes On

And as Spring approached, my life in limbo continued pretty much as I have described here. I was kept busy by my attorneys who cheerfully provided a steady stream of legal documents and court filings that I had to sign, copy and return, and by the DOC, which also provided lots of paperwork for me to do to stay in their good graces. I confess I frittered away too much time on the phone just talking with people, though I really needed whatever moral support that gave me. I also wasted too much time sitting in front of the computer answering emails or playing video games, as well as watching too much TV, but honestly, there was not much else that I could really do.

I crafted a new resume for myself and began looking for any jobs I could find in accounting or bookkeeping, although I wasn't particularly optimistic about my chances of being hired. After all, who's going to hire a convicted felon to manage or oversee their financial books—even though my alleged crime had nothing to do with being dishonest? That's the really insidious problem of labeling someone, and an obstacle that I would come up against time and time again; as a convicted felon when I was still on parole and even now I encounter the stigma, even though, as the cliché goes, I have "paid my debt to society." You label someone a "felon," and to society, that person gets painted with the same brush as the whole spectrum of crimes that constitute the legal definition of "felony," from larceny and embezzlement to violent crimes like physical assault and worse. I was guilty of none of these heinous things, yet most people's concept of the word "felon" said otherwise. But I sent out dozens of applications anyway, and I posted my resume to several online job boards in the slim hope that I might find and employer with an open mind, who could see past the label, who could see what my background was and realize that they could get a great accounts manager for a steal!

And on the positive side, I did become more involved with my church. From the very first day I got out of prison, I knew in my heart and soul that I would need some sort of spiritual guidance and support to get through this, and after a pretty extensive search, in September of 2009 I had found a church community within which I was able to feel comfortable, and just as importantly, where I felt I was accepted for who I was, and not judged for my past nor for the fact that I had just spent significant time in prison. Most importantly to me, the community seemed to welcome me without prejudice, and from the start, I didn't feel like an outsider. The congregation, which is still there, is led by Pastor Tom and his wife, two very kind and compassionate people. And yet, despite all of this acceptance, it was still hard for me. As much as I wanted to go to church every Sunday, because of my deep fear and anxiety and depression, I often stayed home, in my place, where it was safe.

Over time, I became good friends with Pastor Tom and his wife, as well as becoming closer to some members of the congregation, and the pastor became a tremendous source of support and encouragement to carry on despite all of the negativity from the state, all the legal difficulties, and the general depression and abandonment I felt. Slowly but surely I began to participate more actively in church functions and activities. I began cooking meals for church events; brunches, breakfasts, dinners—whatever they needed. I'm a pretty good cook, and this gave me an opportunity to show off my skills. It's funny, but knowing that I had to cook a meal for the church on a given day was often the best motivator of all to make me get up out of bed and get my day started. With Pastor Tom's gentle encouragement, I also began attending weekly Bible study classes, and I helped out with some of the usual church functions. For example, I sometimes acted as pallbearer when one was needed for the family of a departed community member. Without consciously realizing it, there were times when I was so busy with things at the church that I could, for a while at least, forget about my own troubles with the DOC and my unending legal battle with Stoner in Maine.

During this time I also kept plugging away at writing my memoir, though it was slow going. I had been back and forth with numerous literary agents and publishers, many of whom initially expressed sometimes excited interest in publishing my book when it was complete, but all of whom had eventually come back using phrases like, "not what we're looking for at this time," or, "doesn't really suit our publishing list." Still, I am a man who starts what he finishes, so I resolved to persevere and continue writing. Writing a memoir, after all, I realized was something the state, the DOC, and my parole officer could not stop me from doing, even if they didn't like it. Moreover, writing it could, in a real way, be my one act of defiance and rebellion against the system that they couldn't take away from me, or "violate" me for vis-à-vis my "conditions of parole." As a means of keeping track of what was going on in my life, and as potential material for my book, I began and ended every single day by manually jotting down a new entry in my daily journal, a spiral notebook in which I was keeping track of everything, important or trivial, that was happening to me. And I often picked up that journal several times during the day, when I was home, to write down a thought or a new observation, or even simply one more mundane thing I'd done that day.

In late March as I was about to get in the shower, I looked at myself in the mirror and realized I was getting fat! One thing that had almost imperceptibly dropped out of my daily routine was going to the gym to work out, and it was taking a toll on the physical shape I was in, which was none too good! That morning I resolved to do something about my diet, but I wound up doing something that turned out to be even more beneficial not just to reducing my weight, but also to my psychological well-being and emotional outlook on life: I started going out walking, and of course Spring in Alaska was the perfect time to start doing that. The walks got longer and longer, and eventually they evolved into considerably long hikes in the fabulous state parks and forest preserves all around Anchorage that lay within my proverbial "cage" of the Matanuska–Susitna Borough. Often Jim Lewis would go with me (that is when he wasn't back in jail for drunkenness or some such nuisance offense) to Chugach State Park, or along Seward Highway, or up to South Fork State Park in Eagle River and we'd hike together. But a lot of times I would hike the mountains alone, and by mid-May I was hiking 16 miles or longer through some pretty rough terrain and fantastic mountain vistas.

I started bringing my camera along with me, and in fact, the photographs that appear on the dustcover of my book *Derailed* were taken by Jim or me on those long, invigorating hikes through the rugged mountains. Much as I wanted to leave Alaska at the time, I will say this: the breathtaking, heart-pounding panorama that can be seen from her majestic peaks ought to make it utterly impossible for anyone to stay depressed for very long! Those celestial views of endless natural beauty soothed my mind and soul every time, despite all my troubles and worries. After these hikes I would arrive home exhausted and physically sore, but psychologically and spiritually uplifted and energized.

Meanwhile, back on Earth—or shall I say back in the world of mankind and society—my next appointment with my PO was scheduled for April 8th. I arrived early, as I always did, but, once again, Officer Nagyetevi did not show up. At this point, if I hadn't met him "in the flesh" in March, I believe I would have begun to suspect that he didn't actually exist at all; I'd have probably started playing around with the letters in "Zsoly Nagyetevi" to see it might be some secret anagram for something else. In any case, I wound up talking with Sergeant Foster, who said he was the Unit Manager. As I did at every one of my meetings or polygraph appointments, or any time I had interaction with the parole officers or the DOC in general, I asked about the status of my transfer application, and just as every previous time I had asked this question, Officer Foster responded accordingly that there had been "no word from Ohio." Same message, different messenger. So we went over a few trivial things, and he set my next appointment for the 6th of May. I went home thinking that perhaps I should revise my resumé to apply for the job of Parole Officer. Based on what I seen in the job performances of Officers' Nagyetevi and Matthews, you actually didn't need to show up for work, and if you actually choose to do so, you weren't actually obliged to do anything in the way of work!

To my astonishment, Officer Nagyetevi did show up for our appointment in May. I asked the same question about my status, he provided the same answer, end of story for the month on May. I was back home less than two hours after I'd left for the meeting, which is indicative, let me say, of how pointless the meeting was, though in some sense that could be said for most if not all of my meetings with my various parole officers.

Then, on about June 10th, I got a strange, cryptic clue that something was actually happening. I guess I should not have been surprised that it came in the form of an invoice from the State of Ohio, in the amount of $240.00. That night I happened to be going to a Bible study class and prayer meeting at the church, and I prayed that this bill from Ohio betokened the small measure of deliverance I had been seeking for nearly a year now. Initially, I speculated that the invoice represented some sort of processing fee for my transfer to Ohio. There were always fees associated with just about everything I did where it concerned the state government or the DOC in Alaska—I'm surprised I didn't have a *"breathing fee"*—so it would not have been the least bit surprising (rather, it would be expected!) if there was yet another fee for the privilege of being transferred to another state, whether that fee was issued by the sending or the receiving state. (Who knew? Perhaps both states could have their own fee for arranging and processing the transfer!)

Notwithstanding the fee (what's more money down the drain?), it was a tantalizing thought that this invoice represented my ticket home, but I had had my hopes burned many times before, so it's arrival only served to heighten my anxiety and my sense of urgency to get definitive word from somebody in "authority" that the transfer to Ohio had actually been approved.

As I had already learned, getting "definitive" word from someone in authority was a task in itself. At the DOC in Alaska, as I suspect is probably true with every DOC in every state in America, no one tells you anything because everyone engages in a policy of "CYA" (i.e., "Cover Your Ass!").

The next day I tried repeatedly to call the parole office in Ohio only to get their voicemail, and I couldn't even leave a message because the recording deadpanned repeatedly, "The mailbox is full." I sent an email to Officer Nagyetevi asking if he had heard anything, though I fully expected that he would not even bother to respond, which of course proved to be accurate. I resolved to try to be patient, which was the only thing I could do under the circumstances. My next meeting with Nagyetevi (and my next polygraph exam) was June 14th, just three days later—surely I would learn my fate then, would I not?

Wrong again. As if to further my aggravation, Officer Nagyetevi failed to show up again, and he was the only person, apparently, who was authorized to tell me about what, if anything, was happening—that's how "CYA" works! Thus, just to back up a bit, of the six scheduled meetings with my new PO over the first half of 2010, he appeared at only two of them. Oh, I took my polygraph exam alright, and I passed easily as usual, although I wanted to get out of the chair and smash the machine to bits and demand an answer to my one burning question: "Am I getting out of here or what?!" But I just didn't want to have to pay for a new machine along with everything else I was paying for! Incredibly, I went home without any answers. I had a bill in my hand from the State of Ohio; I had no idea what it was for, and nobody in the parole office in Alaska would tell me what it was for, though I suspected that *somebody* there ought to know!

The next day was a Tuesday, and I called Officer Nagyetevi first thing in the morning and, as always, left a message on his voicemail. When he failed to return my call that morning, I called again and left another message at just after 1:00 pm. Finally, about an hour later, he called me back to tell me that my transfer had been approved. Honestly, as happy and relieved as I was to hear it, it was as anticlimactic a moment as I have ever experienced in my life. To be sure, I was very pleased that I would finally be allowed to go home, but it had just taken so much wrangling effort, and it had taken so damn long to get to this point.

There is one last footnote to the story of the $240.00 invoice from the Ohio DOC. As it turned out, it was not some sort of processing fee entailed in my transfer. Rather, in the state of Ohio, parolees are required to pay the state for their own supervision. That $240.00 invoice was my bill from the state of Ohio for supervising me, ostensibly, for the month of June, and I would shortly receive another one for the month of July. Of course, I was still in Alaska, and would be until I could get my affairs in order and leave at the end of July.

Think about that. In June, Ohio was already charging me the monthly fee for being "supervised" as a parolee there, even though I wasn't even physically in the state, and thus of course hadn't yet registered with the parole authorities there. But what that also meant was that my long sought transfer obviously had been approved some time prior to the issuance of the invoice—in May, perhaps, or even sooner. Yet no one at the Alaska DOC parole office bothered to tell me about it. In fact, to this day, I do not know the exact date on which my transfer was actually approved. What I do know is that I was out of pocket $480.00 for "supervision fees" for June and July, before I even set foot in the state of Ohio.

As infuriating as this latest insult was, there really was no time to dwell on it. I now had a lot of things to do and not a lot of time to do them in. Of course, the first thing I did was call my parents to give them the good news. Next I called my landlords to give them notice that I would be out of the apartment at the end of July. I realized I would need to buy some big boxes so that I could start packing, which I did that very evening. I thought about selling my cars, and about holding some yard sales to get rid of all of the stuff that I did not want to keep any longer, or to bother to take with me to Ohio. One of the things that I most wanted to get rid of was the depressive malaise that had plagued me for all these years, in jail and on parole, since this whole nightmare began, and I fervently hoped to leave that in Alaska. Finally, something positive had happened for me. I hoped it was a harbinger of better days ahead as I shut the apartment door behind me and headed off to Wal-Mart in search of sturdy packing boxes.

CHAPTER 5
BE CAREFUL WHAT YOU WISH FOR

Leaving Alaska

In July I advertised a couple of moving sales at which I managed to sell off a good deal of my possessions and furniture that I no longer wanted or needed. Whatever didn't go in the moving sales I donated to ARC of Alaska. I owned two vehicles, one of which was a Dodge Durango that I had purchased so that my parents (as well as Uncle Roger and other visitors) had something to drive around Anchorage when they visited—in particular that first month or so that they had stayed with me after I was first released from prison. The other was the 2009 535 XI BMW that I had gifted to myself when I got out, as I wanted to do something just for me for a change.

I put both up for sale on Craig's list and in the classifieds of the Anchorage Daily News. The Durango sold pretty quickly, the BMW not so much, but actually, that was okay with me. The car was, after all, one of the very few things I had ever so self-indulgently bought just for myself. For a brief time I had a sort of fantasy vision of packing up the Beamer with only those things that were important enough to me to go to the trouble of taking them to Ohio, and embarking by car, somewhat triumphantly, on the nearly 4,000 mile journey from Anchorage to Ashland, free from the watchful eyes of my parole board handlers, and enjoying the peace and solitude of the open road, especially the exquisite beauty of the Canadian back-country. The vision was short-lived.

Because as I sat in the parole office filling out the necessary approval transfer papers for the DOC for Alaska, I realized that, owing to my status as a registered sex offender, I might well have to report my presence to law enforcement authorities all along my travel route. While the trip could have mostly taken me through Canada, depending on the route chosen—where I suspected there was likely little or no requirement to report, much less some Mounty or Constable available to report to—I would still have to travel through a minimum of five U.S. states to get to Ohio. Would I have to report to authorities in every one of those states? What if I had to spend a night in a hotel in some town or city in one or more of those states? I certainly wasn't going to drive 4,000 miles nonstop. I couldn't imagine subjecting myself to such a bureaucratic nightmare, so I quickly dispatched with a sigh the idea of driving home on my own.

Instead I bought a one-way airline ticket for the 28th of July, and when it became clear that the BMW wasn't going to sell, I made arrangements to have it shipped to Ohio. Even with that, I had to file my travel plans with the DOC and provide them with a copy of the airline ticket. I half-assumed that I would get a police escort so that they could make sure I went directly to Ohio and didn't attempt to parachute out of the plane over the Northwestern wilderness like D.B. Cooper. Of course up to that point, all of my experience with traveling under the supervision or jurisdiction of law enforcement had occurred when there had been a warrant out for my arrest—or when I was regarded as a "fugitive" from justice, if you can imagine such a thing—through which I had also learned how much police officers like to use those shiny handcuffs they all carry on their belts. So how was I to know what they would want me to do? And for that reason, I was a little surprised, to say the least, when all Officer Nagyetevi said in our final meeting was, "Get your flight, and report to the parole office in Ohio immediately upon your arrival." And that was it. I flew home to Ohio on July 28, 2010, one year and one month after I got out of prison.

You Can't Go Home Again

Earlier I said that hope is a curious and irrational thing. The same might also be said for our perceptions and memories, and more particularly for what seems to me to be our expectations for permanence in our own little worlds. By that I mean that we seem to implicitly expect that things never change, that the places of our youth are today pretty much exactly the way they were when we left them, or as we remember them—more or less—and that we will easily recognize them should we choose to go back some day. But of course, nothing is further from the truth.

I think that the plane tires had barely scorched the tarmac at Port Columbus International Airport before I began, somewhat incredulously after nearly a year of begging and pleading with authorities to get here, to question whether I was doing the right thing. In fact, it's almost embarrassing to admit it, but my journal entry for my first full day back in Ashland ends with the lines, "It is good to be home but I really don't know if I will stay or go back to Alaska. I have to give it a chance here." The reality was that I was returning to my "home" in semi-urban, urbane Ohio after 20 years of living in an utterly different milieu in the state of Alaska, where many of the people are as rugged and rough-edged as that state's mountain wilderness itself. In other words, Ohio had really not been my home for over 20 years, and by returning, I was plunged into a completely different sort of social environment than I had known for all of that time.

Moreover, I was a 50-year-old man coming back to live in his parents' home, though that was certainly not my choice, but rather necessitated by my offender status and the good folks at DOC. Mind you, I love both my parents very much, and they had supported me throughout all of my legal battles, through my incarceration, and through all of my personal troubles for all of these past several years. But I was soon to learn the lesson that, sometimes, "family" isn't always what it's cracked up to be, but even more than that, living in a little too much uneasy proximity to family—specifically, under the same roof—can be a nightmare!

It would be a colossal understatement to say that Mom and Dad were set in their ways. Approaching their 70s, and married for nearly 50 of those years, they had adopted and fine-tuned, like married couples do, a unique and sometimes bizarre manner of getting along and working out their disputes that would have made the Hatfield's and the McCoy's proud. At no time was this "symbiosis" more apparent than, for instance, during their monthly skirmishes to balance the checkbook. Dad had his idiosyncratic way of doing it, Mom had her own peculiar method, and as if stubbornness was a virtue, then to their mutual credit it was quite apparent to me that neither had yielded an inch over the past 50 years. If I tried to interfere by offering some sound financial or accounting advice—which I happen to be pretty good at—it only made matters worse, so I soon learned that the best thing to do was to butt out and retreat to my room until the firefight was over. Of course, they were both genuinely happy to see me and have me home, or so it seemed, and for the first month or so life was happy and halcyon. However, it would not be long before certain aspects of our relationships would begin to deteriorate.

Out of the Frying Pan...

My first responsibility upon arriving in Ohio was to report to the parole office where I was supposed to meet my new PO—one Ilse Bleucher, a woman officer—and I was also required to go the sheriff's office to sign officially into the sex offender registry, and I set out to do so the morning of July 29th, the day after I arrived back in the state. However, when I got the parole office I discovered that Mrs. Bleucher was not in, and I found myself going from office to office, getting the runaround—no one there could or would tell me anything about what I was supposed to do or where I should report. Of course, I was pretty familiar with this sort of inherently dysfunctional, non-communicative DOC bureaucracy back in Alaska, so I guess you could say that I wasn't particularly surprised to find similar disorganization and confusion within the Ohio DOC. I finally managed to reach my new PO by phone, and she instructed me to go see one Officer Clark in the Sheriff's Department, who would help me sign into the sex offender registry. She further instructed to meet her the next morning at 9:00 am at the Ashland Court House on Second Street.

Earlier in this book I was critical of the Alaska Department of Corrections, its parole board and parole officers, and its administration of the state's parole program. That criticism ranged across a wide spectrum of factors: one could start by citing parole officers having a lackadaisical attitude about doing their jobs—best typified by PO Nagyetevi's failure to show up for nearly 70% of our scheduled appointments—or not doing their jobs at all—such as PO Matthews's failure to even bother to file my transfer request. Then there was the lack of specific and clear direction with respect to my so-called "conditions of parole." Both of my POs in Alaska seemed to pick-and-choose which of those conditions they wanted me to adhere to, and which ones, to use their professional terminology, they didn't "give a shit" about whether I followed the rules or not.

Of course, the worst of all was the way that the parole board categorically refused to allow me to try to get back into a productive business; one that would enable me to pick up the pieces and move on with my life, make some money to put food on the table, but at the same time, a business that would also benefit the community at large, which was an important part of what I wanted to achieve. This recalcitrant and unyielding policy posture begins right in the prisons themselves, where there are absolutely no programs to help inmates find work or start a career—to start their lives over in a meaningfully productive and law-abiding way—once they've done their time and are released. (This is an issue that I talked about in greater detail in *Derailed*.) And this continues when they get out, when ex-cons are prohibited from engaging in so many work, career, and business opportunities through which they might actually be able to "get back on their feet," to become productive members of their communities and of society in general—either once again, as in my case, or for the first time, as might have been the case for so many of the young inmates I met during my stay in Palmer Correctional who had made serious mistakes so early in life. The effort—and the critical need in this country—to bring an end to this intolerable attitude and to these unacceptable circumstances and restrictions of freedom is the main thrust of this book, and I will have more to say about this in the text that follows. As for the loose and sometimes seemingly laissez-faire application of the parole conditions in Alaska, I should perhaps have considered myself lucky. Because it got much, much worse in Ohio, where it seemed like my every movement was being monitored and recorded.

In short, the parole board and the sheriff's department in Ohio seemed to want to know my whereabouts at all times; they were intent and determined to know what I was doing or planning to do with my time all the time, and they demanded to know where I might be planning to travel ahead of time, which they might approve or not approve—sometimes approving one week, but denying permission the next. I felt as though I was constantly running back and forth to the parole office to get travel passes to Columbus or Cleveland, for example, or particularly on occasions when I needed or wanted to go out of state. Moreover, my "cage" had gotten much, much smaller. In Alaska, I had the City of Anchorage and all of Matanuska–Susitna Borough where I could roam freely, over 61,000 square miles of territory, and in hindsight I suspect that if I had ever strayed out of the Borough, whether deliberately or by accident, my parole officer would never have been able to find out about it, and even if he did, I seriously doubt he would have cared. After all, wherever one might have strayed out of the Borough would have probably been nothing but more wilderness anyway. Compare that vast rural expanse with tiny Ashland County, Ohio, which is 427 square miles, with the one lousy, economically depressed city of Ashland, population just over 20,000, and you may get a sense of the virtual claustrophobia I was now feeling. Anchorage, by contrast, is a bustling, vibrant, economically powerful metropolis with a population of just under 300,000 people; comprising an area of 1,691 square miles, the city alone is roughly four and a half times as big as all of Ashland County Ohio!

So intrusive was my parole officer's monitoring of my life and my daily activities that I began to worry about even the most harmless of pursuits. For example, in January of 2011, the Ashland Symphony Orchestra gave a concert at the local high school. I was invited by some friends and I wanted to go, but as perfectly harmless as going to a concert should seem to be, I was genuinely afraid to do so without the express permission of my parole officer. That may seem silly and absurd; that is, until you consider the facts that the concert was held at a school, and, as a registered sex offender, I am prohibited from going anywhere near a school. Would I be in violation if I attended the evening concert—held at a time when classes were not in session? The answer to that question was quite unclear to me, and I did not wish to take any chances, so in the days leading up to the event, I called my parole officer and left messages asking for permission to attend. I would have sent her some email messages, except that I was not allowed to send emails to parole officers or to the parole office, although I had been allowed to do that back in Alaska. Of course, as was so typical in Alaska, and no different in Ohio, I got no response whatsoever to my inquiries. Still fearing the possibility of committing a parole violation that might send me back to prison, the concert date came and went and I stayed home.

Now this, I submit, is the way fear and paranoia are generated, and indeed, cultivated to a purpose in a police state. In an authoritarian regime, the goal of the government is to make the people fearful, even terrified, of doing anything that might be construed as "stepping out of line" and subject to arbitrary arrest without recourse to legal right of appeal through the courts. This is precisely as Thomas Jefferson stated it when he said, "When the people fear their government, there is tyranny; when the government fears the people, there is liberty." I argue throughout this book that, tragically and outrageously, in America today, the former is ever-increasingly the rule.

But I want to take this discussion even further by emphasizing that last part: subject to *arbitrary arrest without recourse to legal right of appeal* through the courts, which was very specific, and a key, to my situation. What I have learned about being on parole in these United States is that it is precisely like being a citizen under a dictatorship as terrible and oppressive as the Third Reich or the former Soviet Union. As a parolee in America, I had virtually no freedom of movement or of association, and I was effectively stripped of the rights that Americans claim to hold so dear, and which are embodied in our Constitution—a Constitution, I would argue, that is being slowly disemboweled as I write this book.

Think about that: As a citizen, I was too afraid to attend a simple, benign orchestra performance in a publically owned, taxpayer-supported institution. And in the end I never got an answer to the question as to whether it would have been okay to do so. Because when I raised the issue again, complaining mildly to my PO after the concert had happened, she said cavalierly, "Well, I guess it really doesn't matter now, since the concert is over." Nice.

But there was even more fun in store for me here. Upon registering as a resident in Ohio I was immediately required to enroll in a "sex offender education" course that was held every Monday afternoon in Mansfield, running for about 22 or 23 weeks, as I recall. In this unique and rather curious course we were supposed to talk about our feelings and emotions, and the instructor pontificated on the socially acceptable—and unacceptable—ways of dealing with those feelings. We were given actual homework to do—or else, naturally and predictably—be deemed in violation of parole if we failed to complete it each week. So I always studiously did my homework and turned it in on time. They even held an official "graduation," complete with photographs of the smiling graduates, the instructors, and some local politicians, for the newspapers naturally, so that the DOC could show the public how wisely and successfully they were using taxpayer dollars to reform sexual offenders.

And as if all of that wasn't enough, unlike Alaska, Ohio greeted me back home by printing up a flyer with my picture on it, and identifying me as a Registered Sex Offender, and placing one in the mailboxes of all of my neighbors within whatever radius is prescribed by law. I was so ashamed and heartbroken to be reminded that I would have to carry that insidious label around for the rest of my life, even though I had never in my life lifted a finger to hurt anyone.

My parole officer, Ms. Bleucher, was a rude, irresponsible, disrespectful, power-tripping tyrant. Back in Alaska, I had gotten ticked off, periodically about once a month, when my PO failed to show up for our appointments, or when an appointment or a scheduled polygraph test was abruptly rescheduled to a different day and time with neither adequate notice nor the courtesy of an explanation. In hindsight, I should have been grateful for Alaska's lack of functional diligence. Because in Ohio, PO Bleucher very deliberately and very effectively raised this genre of interpersonal insult and disrespect to an art form. She thought nothing of calling me up in the afternoon or even in the evening to order me to be in her office the following morning—the very next day—at say, 9:00am sharp for a meeting, without any concern or consideration as to whether I might have something important to do that day, or some obligation to meet. At the same time, much like PO Nagyetevi in Alaska, she had no compunction whatsoever about simply not showing up herself for prescheduled meetings, leaving me with yet another wasted day on which I might have done something—anything—more productive.

Sometimes when I arrived at her office for an appointment in the morning, at say 9 or 10 o'clock, she'd tell me she was too busy and order me to come back at 2 or 3 in the afternoon. With any other plans I may have had for the day now in a shambles, there was little or nothing constructive I could accomplish, except to either wait around the parole office, or go home and return to the office in the afternoon. Another day shot as to productivity. Other times I'd arrive to find a note on her locked office door with one word on it: "OUT." No other explanation, no other instruction as to whether I should report to anyone else, or what else I should do next. If I had the temerity to complain to PO Bleucher that this disruptive and utterly unpredictable way of overseeing my "case" was making it difficult (to put it mildly) for me to productively plan my time or to do anything constructive (think: doing constructive things toward, possibly, my "rehabilitation," if you will), I was brusquely—and rudely—told that it was simply my responsibility to know when and where I was supposed to meet with my parole officer, that I had to go to my sex offender class, and, in effect, that I had to do whatever else I was ordered to do by the parole board or the sheriff's department, whenever and wherever they ordered me to do it. And that I should shut up about it. I was flat out told by PO Bleucher—and others for that matter—that I had no freedoms and I had no legal rights, except for those which the PO herself, or the board, or the sheriff, decided out of their great sense of benevolence they would give me—and which they might just as easily retract if they felt like it.

This, the last time I checked, was—and still is—happening in America. And if PO Bleucher needed any further validation of her absolute power and authority over me (and all of her other parolee charges as well), she could easily find it in the happy coincidence that she happened to be the wife of Ashland's Chief of Police. Ultimately, she ran me ragged with confusing and conflicting instructions and orders; with cancelled, postponed, and rescheduled appointments and meetings; with numerous unannounced visits to inspect my parents' home; and with her smug, dictatorial and imperiously superior attitude that belied her apparent utter contempt for me as a person, much less as a rightful citizen. I was the animal; she was the trainer with all of the hoops and barrels she could order me to jump through and over. In my view, she was, and remains, a despicable and vindictive person in love with her own sense of power, and an utter disregard for the welfare of her parolee charges.

But what I came to realize in all of this, much to my horror and dismay, was that I had left a state where, whether through incompetence or ineptitude—or just possibly, through a more laid-back and even a more practical, self-reliant, and humanistic attitude and approach—parolees are given a little bit more "slack," a little more latitude and self-responsibility—and yes, even a measure of respect—to a state where parole supervision is conducted in militaristic but arbitrary fashion, in which parolees are entirely stripped of their constitutional rights, and worst of all, one in which there is no human respect whatsoever for the persons in the parole system mill. This considerable disparity in the way I was treated—and in the way the rules were interpreted between the two states—resulted in my first "write up" on parole, a kind of "parole violation warning," not unlike the written warning you might get from a traffic cop who mercifully decides not to write you an actual ticket.

PO Bleucher was fond of showing up, often and always unannounced of course, at the door of my parents' home for an inspection of the house and in particular, my quarters. In the course of these inspections she might commandeer documents, bills, phone records, computer file printouts, books—my journals from time to time (so I had to be very careful about what I wrote in there!), or even my wallet and cell phone—and just about anything else her little heart desired, to take with her back to her office for closer inspection, and to be returned later. Lest you think "commandeer" too strong or suggestive a term, or that I am being unfair in using it, yes, in a strict sense you're right; she was required by law to always ask to "borrow" these items rather than "demand" that I turn them over. However, as condition of my parole, I was nonetheless always obliged to surrender them or (if you'll forgive the broken record), I would be in "violation" of my parole. So let's not mince words: If PO Bleucher wanted to confiscate these items, she took them. I really had no say in the matter. Period.

It was on one such visit that Bleucher discovered a letter from Jim Lewis, who at the time he authored it, was lodged in Anchorage jail again, the return address plainly disclosing that fact on the outside of the envelope for all to see. Nor was it any great Sherlockian feat of detective sleuthing on her part—the letter was sitting right there, out in the open in plain sight, on top of the writing desk in my room. After all, my PO in Alaska had effectively given me permission to talk to or correspond with anyone I wanted, including the villains, thieves, and scoundrels with whom I had become friends "in the joint." But an indignant PO Bleucher, who was clearly very satisfied with herself for making this shocking "find," confiscated the letter and reported it to her boss, and for this, I received my first official disciplinary action; a parole violation write up. Something that my parole officer in Alaska said he, "didn't give a shit about," got me in trouble with my parole officer in Ohio, who made it abundantly clear that she was going to "give a shit" about every niggling little thing I could possibly do wrong in her eyes—and that was just about everything and anything.

When I had finally gotten my transfer to Ohio, I was informed that I would have to abide by the "conditions of parole" in *both* states. Nobody ever told me, however, which state's rules should prevail when the two DOC authorities are in direct contradiction with one another. What's a parolee to do? When I appealed to PO Bleucher, pointing out that when I was in Alaska I had been allowed by my parole officer there to correspond with, and even associate with Jim and other people who were still "in the system," she responded cold and callously, "Well, you're not in Alaska anymore." I suppose I could have predicted that response.

The incident over Jim Lewis's letter and the big hullabaloo that ensued over it was probably the first time that the thought arose in me, of just packing in this whole parole thing and requesting that the DOC simply send me back to Palmer Correctional to finish out the rest of my sentence in prison, where frankly, it was a lot easier to follow the damn rules. In prison parlance, this is called "flat-timing." What I was doing by corresponding with Jim and others was so pathetically innocuous; it wasn't as though we could even so much as have an illicit beer together in a bar somewhere, perhaps planning a bank heist, what with being separated by 4,000 miles. I hadn't even made any attempt whatsoever to be secretive or subversive about it—in part because I regarded it as so harmless as to not be a bother to anyone—but mainly because my parole officers in Alaska already knew about my relationship with Jim and did not care anything about it; had in fact, for all intents and purposes, told me it was okay. Yet the repercussions came anyway from PO Bleucher, and she acted as though I had robbed a liquor store at gunpoint. It wasn't that a parole violation write-up was "severe" as punishments go, but it was the principle: it was all just so patently unfair and in my view, a gross misuse of power.

1,825 DAYS OF HELL: ONE MAN'S ODYSSEY THROUGH THE AMERICAN PAROLE SYSTEM

...And Out of the Workplace

And yet, in the scheme of things, the reprimand over the Jim Lewis letter was trivial. Because by far, the most disturbing aspect of this overhanded, deliberately disruptive supervision was that it effectively removed any possibility of my holding down any sort of decent job in which keeping a routine schedule would be required, which of course, includes any kind of purposeful employment, full or part time. Forget about any thoughts of starting up and running my own business or franchise, which would require working 14 hours a day six or seven days a week. Just the very idea of doing even a typical 9-to-5 office job, or for that matter an irregular part time job, say, nights and weekends, was unthinkable, because at any given hour of any given day (or night), I might get a call out of the blue from my parole officer, and I would have to put down the ledger books or "hang up the apron" to go meet with her, or to report to the parole office for some other ridiculous trumped-up reason. Under such circumstances, there would be times I'd have to tell my boss on the spot that I have to leave, or that I would not be able to come in on time the following day—or at all—and no employer is going to put with that kind of nonsense for very long, nor should they have to. PO Bleucher clearly operated on the philosophy that the best way to keep her parolees in line and on their toes—in her little mind, to keep them from getting into more mischief—was to keep them constantly disrupted, constantly guessing what she was going to do next, and constantly at her beck and call like a bunch of lap dogs. What she tragically failed to realize was that such a policy also very effectively makes it impossible for them to even attempt to become productive members of society again.

Or, I have another theory. Which is that PO Bleucher and her colleagues know only too well the ramifications of the intrusive, overbearing, and Gestapo-like supervisory model that has become the sad hallmark of our modern day parole systems in the U.S. Undeniably, the effective consequence of their actions—and what we as Americans who believe in freedom and justice should be most outraged about—is that parolees simply are left with no reasonable possibility of maintaining a daily routine of regular, gainful employment as a means of getting back on their feet and becoming a productive member of society, much less making a decent living, and this is the case for millions of parolees all across this country. It is the reason that less than half of all of the millions of parolees in America actually succeed in making it through the parole system to freedom at all, with over 50 percent of them being returned to prison—a large percentage of them not because they commit new crimes, but simply for minor parole violations!

And of course, by keeping people "in the system," PO Bleucher and her cronies are quite effectively able to ensure and perpetuate their own ultimate form of job security. Every failed parolee sent back to prison validates the reason for existence for DOCs and parole boards, and the hiring or employment of thousands of corrections and parole officers, as well as "validating" the spending of billions of dollars of public money to support these people and their institutions, and it's all a self-fulfilling, revolving-door system that feeds on itself; a dragon with its tail in its mouth.

I will have much more to say about the dysfunctional state of the parole system and its operations, and the U.S. correctional system in general, in Chapter 8 of this book, backed by facts and figures from several sources, including such reputable ones as our own U.S. Bureau of Justice Statistics.

But let me make a forthright acknowledgment here, which is to say, yeah, I get it. As a parolee still under the supervision of the state DOC (whichever state that happens to be), I should expect to be jerked around a little bit. Some skeptical people, and certainly the cynical ones, undoubtedly would argue that I deserved it. After all, I was convicted, right? Then I was "graciously" granted the "privilege" of living outside of prison walls, among presumably law-abiding citizens, instead of having to spend my days locked away with a bunch of cons in "the big house." What a treat. (Never mind that a large part of parole is specifically to ease prison overcrowding which is, cyclically in turn, largely due to this failed parole system—that dragon eating its tail again.)

But you have to ask yourself some serious questions. First, what does the state gain by jerking me and the millions of other parolees around in this way, making it impossible for us to get decent jobs and maintain gainful employment? A huge tax bill, perhaps? And second, is it too much to ask that our government instead devise ways to provide opportunities for employment so that these people begin paying taxes themselves, instead of being stuck in a system that simply sucks those tax dollars up? And finally, which of those options do you think accords more with the democratic ideal in America? After all: It is supposed to be the "Department of Corrections"; it is not called the "Department of Incarcerations."

From my viewpoint, I had done nothing criminal or against the law, but I was forced to take a plea bargain because, my attorneys assured me, I would not receive a fair trial in the municipal court where the hearing would be conducted, and the judge and prosecutor refused to grant a change of venue to another court where I could. They weren't interested in justice: they wanted to look "tough on crime" and notch another victorious conviction on their respective belts. Certainly, it should be clear to anyone that as a gay man in the midst of a predominately evangelical, Christian-conservative population, I wasn't going to face a "jury of my peers"—not even a mosaic of jurors that might include a few members among my peers. But in the state's eyes, of course, a plea deal is tantamount to a conviction, case closed. So be it.

So what's my point? My point is that the serious problem with all if this is that, despite being wrongfully accused and wrongfully convicted, I fully accepted my fate and I strove to play by the rules. In prison, I was a model inmate intent on earning parole release as soon as I was eligible; on the outside, I diligently studied my "conditions of parole" and just as diligently endeavored to follow them strictly to the letter, even as they were administered by different parole officers and boards in wildly inconsistent and often contradictory terms. I had been forced to acknowledge, to myself and to the court, that I had probably made some mistakes of judgment that only served to put me in the predicament I was in (though notwithstanding, in my heart and my soul, I never did anything wrong or intended to hurt anyone), and I had dutifully accepted the consequences even though I shall maintain for the rest of my life that those consequences were far more dreadful than I deserved.

And that, specifically, is the point. I could accept being monitored by the DOC and required to report to my parole officer from time to time, on a regular schedule; I could accept, as personally hurtful and psychologically debilitating as it was, having to register as a sex offender within whatever jurisdiction that I desired to live in. What I could absolutely not accept then, and still cannot accept today, was the authorities' abject and categorical refusal to allow me the opportunity to get back on my business horse, perhaps even start a new company that would create jobs for people, and more pointedly to become a productive member of society again. I wanted to do good—for myself, for my family, for my community and even beyond—and they wouldn't let me. That, to me, is an American tragedy.

A Moot Point

Maybe all of this was much ado about nothing. Because, quite sadly, with or without these onerous restrictions on my activities and travels, the hard reality is that, in practical terms, I think it is accurate to say that it was highly unlikely I was going to find decent, meaningful employment, much less actually be able to start up a new business in this part of Ohio, by any stretch of the imagination. And that's not sour grapes, either. One of the disturbing things that struck me rather powerfully not long after I returned was how economically depressed the whole state had become—or really, how depressed it had remained—since I first left it. How, I wondered, had I so completely forgotten how bad thing were economically here in my home state?

What was incredible about my apparent memory lapse was that the poor economy and the lack of opportunity for an ambitious youth was one of the main reasons I *left* Ohio in the first place, 20 years earlier, and struck out for Alaska. Driving around the town of Ashland, the memories all came roaring back like a blow right between the eyes! I had a déjà vu moment separated by two decades—this place hadn't changed at all; if anything, its economic plight had only gotten worse, if that was imaginable! Like the rest of the nation, Ohio had been hit hard by the economic meltdown of 2008. In 1987 when I left, my father had a good job with Abbott Laboratories, which had their giant Plastics Division facility in Ashland, where they manufactured all sorts of intravenous tubing and plastic surgical and medical plastic equipment for hospitals across the country. My mother worked for F.E. Myers and Bro., which at one time was the biggest manufacturer in Ashland (among no less than 47 factories which flourished in the town in the mid-1800s and early 1900s). F.E. Myers manufactured water pumps and hay harvesting tools. Over the ensuing years while I was building my health care businesses in Alaska and Maine, my mother retired in 2000 and my father retired in 2002.

However, when I returned in 2010, F.E. Myers and Bro. was gone, and so was the Abbott Labs facility, now a massive, vacant complex surrounded by a rusting chain-link fence with chains and padlocks on the sad-looking, dilapidated gates. Furthermore, Ashland lies on the I-71–I-76 corridor a mere 50 miles from Akron, an area that once billed itself as the "Rubber Capital of the World," but which now was a region that had simply hit the skids. Commercial buildings and storefronts throughout the city of Ashland—the County Seat, mind you—were boarded up; the only place one could buy clothing, or any other regular household goods for that matter, was at the one remaining store, WalMart. Picture this: Whenever I wanted to purchase a decent suit or some clothing just a little more upscale than what one typically finds at WalMart, I had to go to Mansfield or Columbus where they still had a Macy's and some other department stores that carried the better merchandise. And of course, I had to get permission from my PO to travel there, because both cities are located out of Ashland County. Thus, in effect, I had to ask permission to go clothes shopping! Do you get the claustrophobic man-in-a-cage picture now?

And yet, I have never been one to shrink from a difficult challenge, particularly when it comes to business. Regardless of the obstacles that were placed in front of me and despite the dubiousness of whether the state would actually allow me to either start a business or to go to work in some capacity I kept trying to find something I could do. I investigated and pursued dozens of leads on potential opportunities—so many that I can't even remember them all. I do remember one in particular; a pharmaceutical firm in Connecticut that was in trouble, and

1,825 DAYS OF HELL: ONE MAN'S ODYSSEY THROUGH THE AMERICAN PAROLE SYSTEM

its owner was looking for a partner to help turn it around—something I had already done for I-Care Pharmacy in Maine. Unfortunately, the company was simply drowning in debt, and it was a no-go.

I wrote to state legislators to see if they could help me with my plight, but none did. I should have realized they weren't going to touch a registered sex offender. I went to Ohio's Department of Economic Development. They seemed interested and indicated that they wanted to help, but that there was nothing that they could do to help me. In reality, I believe, they were interested in helping until they learned about my conviction and my status as a felon, and that's when they said that they couldn't help me. Here I was a former CEO with a strong track record of building businesses and—most importantly—creating jobs, talking to a state agency devoted to job creation and economic development for Ohio, and they basically wouldn't work with me, really didn't want anything to do with me. In the end, I am quite certain they were also very uncomfortable about my history and really just wanted me to go away.

As time wore on and I resigned myself to life, or let's just call it "existence" in my parents' home, living with them rapidly became more and more intolerable. Both of them had health issues, and naturally I wanted to help them out as much as I possibly could. I certainly had the time on my hands to do that; that is, when I wasn't running off to PO Bleucher's office. But the more and more work and household chores I did for them, the less and less they did, and the less they appreciated everything I was doing. That first summer I started by doing all of the yard work, mowing the lawn, maintaining the shrubs and flowerbeds, and raking leaves in the Fall. But soon I was doing the laundry—including stripping the beds, washing the sheets, and remaking the beds. I was cleaning the house, doing the food shopping, running errands, making dinner, and just about everything else that goes into running a house.

My mother was a little too fond of wine, and she often spent afternoons or evenings with a glass in her hand talking mindlessly and very loudly on the phone for hours and hours, usually to her sister—and always in the living room where the television was, effectively making it impossible for me or anyone else to actually watch a movie or anything else on TV. Increasingly, my father just sat in his chair shouting orders at both her and me, but mostly at me. Sometimes I couldn't believe how they seemed to treat me as some sort of manservant—a combination butler, maid, chef, and general groundskeeper. And then I found myself paying to replace large appliances that failed or footing the bill for various major home repairs!

Perhaps much of this was my own fault. I have to concede that I have a long history of trying, to excess, to help other people only to have them walk all over me. I've loaned money to people dozens of times that I never got back. I trusted scores of people, from my business (and life!) partner, to my employees and associates, to my attorneys and advisers, and even our U.S. Courts of Justice, only to get screwed by them and taken advantage of in ways that I would never, ever do to another human being. In a real sense, I had let it all happen, over and over again. And here I was being taken advantage of by my very own parents, who seemed not the least bit concerned about what they were doing to me, or to feel bad about the way they were really using me, and I was letting all of that happen, too. I resented it, and day after day I swore, alternatively, that for the sake of my sanity I would get my own place, or that I was going to take the bull by the horns and just go back to Alaska where I belonged. But I did neither. Instead I just suffered through it. Some years later a friend would ask me why, with all the thankless aggravation and grief I was going through, I never just picked up and left. I had only a one word answer. "Family," I sighed.

The tragedy in all of this was that I had my own place, right in town, where I should have been permitted to live. I had bought the house on Center Street, not far from my parents' place, back in 2007 before all of these difficulties began, so that I could have my own place to stay whenever I came back to Ohio to visit them. Because they were both beginning to experience some significant health issues, I believed that I would have to visit them more often, and so buying my own place seemed like a worthwhile and prudent thing to do. (In fact, at one point I looked into the prospect of turning this house into a boarding house, but dropped that idea once I got a look at the ridiculous and unconscionable mountain of state regulations that would need to be met just to open the doors.)

However, the parole board, in its infinite wisdom, ruled that I could not live in the house because they was a small preschool day care center housed in a church basement about a block and a half away, and I, of course, was now a registered sex offender required to keep a "safe" distance away from small children and schools. Actually, the parole board and the sheriff's office had opposing viewpoints on the issue: the parole board led by PO Bleucher insisted I could not live there, while the Sheriff's office said it would be okay. Of course, Bleucher ruled the day, as she always managed to do the entire time I was under her supervision. (I have since learned, now that I am no longer on parole, that the sheriff's opinion was the correct one after all.)

So instead of being able to live in the house on Center Street, I spent several years being forced to try to sell it in one of the worst real estate markets in memory across the entire country, but especially in dying cities like Ashland, all the while paying the mortgage, and the taxes, and the upkeep, on a vacant building.

Indeed, there were many times when I contemplated just letting the bank take the house: Why should I keep paying taxes and the mortgage on a home I wasn't even allowed to live in? And of course, I was constantly running over there to mow the lawn, rake the leaves, shovel the snow, and just generally keep up the maintenance of the place, as I periodically dropped the asking price, begging for a buyer. For a time, I managed to rent the place out to a couple with a small child, but that actually turned out to be an even bigger headache than the vacant building, when I eventually had to take my tenants to court for nonpayment of the rent!

I don't know for certain, but perhaps, had Mom and Dad been in better health, I might have simply picked up and gone back to Alaska. But under the circumstances, I simply couldn't bring myself to do that; it goes against the very grain of everything I believe about the singular importance and the centrality of family in my life, even if your family doesn't treat you with the respect they should, or at least treat you as well as you treat them. As for getting my own place nearby, money of course, was a significant issue. If I had been able to sell the house I was prohibited from living in, I might have been able to buy another one where I could. Nevertheless, I felt trapped. I was trapped in the Ohio parole system, trapped in tiny Ashland County, trapped in the inability to get a job, and trapped in my parents' home, and in a very real sense there was nothing that was actually mine. So I settled unwillingly into a routine daily existence that was even more boring and more mundane—and abominably more unproductive and unfulfilling—than the one I had been living in Alaska. There are no wilderness areas or state forests, or even so much as a decent park in Ashland, just depressing city streets lined with row after row of boarded up factories and deteriorating warehouses, so I stopped the rigorous hiking that I had grown so fond of doing through the mountains surrounding Anchorage.

I used any excuse I could to get out of the house to try to get a little time and space for myself—so that I wouldn't wind up getting trapped in the middle of a confrontation between them during one of their raucous arguments. I had very few friends here, as most of the people I knew from 20 years ago had picked up and left for better opportunities elsewhere in the country, just as I had done. I had some relatives nearby, whom I would visit regularly, or meet somewhere in town for lunch. And I ran errands to town—lots of errands, just so I could be alone in my car and hear myself think.

The Casinos Become my Refuge

Fortunately, or perhaps unfortunately as things would turn out, I found an escape. Both Ohio and nearby Wheeling, West Virginia have casinos. Gambling is one on my guilty pleasures. Strange as it may seem, and what you might expect from its rough-and-tumble, hard-knuckle frontier history, Alaska does not have legalized gambling, so a gambling junket for me back then usually involved a plane ride and a long weekend in Las Vegas where I would meet up with my folks, some friends, or some business associates. That ended as soon as I was convicted and later released on parole, and, as noted previously, my parole officers in Alaska rejected my requests for permission to go to Las Vegas. But here in Ohio, there was an assortment of casinos only a couple of hours' drive from Ashland, and to my quiet astonishment, for all of the harmless things she refused to let me do, PO Bleucher granted me permission to go on overnights and long weekends to the gambling casinos in Columbus, Cleveland and Wheeling. I certainly wasn't going to complain about such good fortune, but I absolutely could not help but be dumbfounded at the striking irony of it all. Remember that among the strict conditions of my parole I was prohibited from drinking alcohol, and I was also prohibited from patronizing any establishments whose "primary business is the dispensing of alcoholic beverages." In fact, never mind "patronizing," the exact wording of the actual parole condition was that I shall not even "enter" such an establishment!

Now quite clearly, the dispensing of alcoholic beverages is certainly not the primary business of the gaming industry. Their business might be more accurately described as providing legalized, state-regulated gambling on games of chance—that's why it's called the "gaming industry." And it is also true that in Ohio and West Virginia the casinos are prohibited from providing alcoholic beverages to their gambling patrons for free, which is allowed in many other states where legalized gambling is allowed. But let's call a spade a spade: anyone who thinks that alcohol and alcohol consumption aren't an integral part of the casino gambling experience or "milieu" still believes in the tooth fairy. While they may not say it openly, casino operators want and encourage their patrons to drink, plain and simple, for reasons that are so obvious that there is no need for me to explain them here. So in a way, it was rather shocking to me that PO Bleucher so matter-of-factly, without much deliberation at all, or so it seemed, approved my numerous requests to visit the casinos both in-state and out of state. And it points once again to the confounding arbitrariness with which my "conditions of parole" were administered in wildly inconsistent, often conflicting ways by different parole officers in different states. Since Alaska does not allow casino gambling, I concede that there is no uniform point of reference here for a direct comparison, and therefore it remains an open question whether my parole officers there would have allowed me to go to a casino if there was legalized gambling in the state. However, they did specifically deny me permission to travel to Las Vegas for the same purpose, and I submit that a fairly sound conclusion may be quite easily and logically drawn from that unequivocal refusal.

I mention all of this as a further example of the head-spinning absurdity of the way my parole was overseen by different people in different jurisdictions—even, I would submit, within the same general jurisdiction. But I started off by saying that the casinos presented a refuge for me, and I certainly wasn't interested in going to them simply so that I could get away with having a surreptitious drink, so let me explain.

The thing about the casino, for me the desirable, almost ethereal quality of the atmosphere that I found there, can be summed up in two words: anonymity and equality. I'll talk about the latter first. Inside the casino, every single person is the same, and every person is stripped right down to being exactly equal to everyone else. You are a purveyor of games of chance, a gambler. No one else cares who you are, what you do for a living, or what sort of good and evil lurks in your past. You can be a Fortune 500 company president or a steelworker, a police officer or a mobster, you can be gay or straight; no one gives a damn. The playing cards, the dice, the roulette wheel, and the slot machine rule; they alone decide the winners and the losers, and of course I've been both, but usually the latter! Beyond that everyone there is equal, everyone there is after the same thing, that big payoff, and certainly, nobody inside a gambling casino is there for the purpose of judging or criticizing anyone else!

It was perhaps because of all of this that whenever I went to the casinos I felt an enormously exhilarating sense of freedom and of being "normal," of being just like everybody else in the room. I felt at last like I could actually breathe, and the air I breathed was like some sort of sweetly natural (and legal!) narcotic. I was no longer, "Jerry Lynn Tanner, Convicted Felon listed on the Sex Offender Registry"; I was just another gambler at the gaming tables trying his luck and hoping to hit it big. Mr. Anonymous. For a few hours, even a couple of days, I could feel like I could let my hair down and I didn't have to be constantly and nervously looking over my shoulder to see who was watching me, waiting for me to screw up again—because absolutely no one was. It was an intensely liberating, mind-freeing experience, almost hallucinogenic in a way. In fact, I guess I would say that it was hallucinogenic, because once I returned to Ashland all of the fears and anxieties and paranoia of the reality of my existence came roaring back with a vengeance. And ultimately, getting one more "hit" of that sweet air of freedom would prove to be my undoing.

CHAPTER 6
WHEN ENOUGH BECOMES TOO MUCH

Revelations and Coming to Terms

So, after only a relatively short time back home, I had come to several sobering realizations, the first of which was that parole supervision in my home state was a veritable gauntlet of restrictions and reporting requirements, perfectly legal but nonetheless insulting home invasions and personal affronts; all in all a continual series of hoops and barrels I had to jump through or over, a whole lot of "No you can'ts," and all far more intrusive and undignified than anything I had experienced in Alaska, although Alaska was no picnic either. I had quickly discovered that moving in with your parents at age 50 is no bowl of cherries either, and that as long as I would have to stay with them, I'd have to get myself out of the house as often as possibly just to preserve what little sanity I believed I had left. While it's true I was all alone, and felt it, in my home in Anchorage, at least I had some privacy and peace of mind. Furthermore, I'd learned—*re*-learned, actually—that the economic and business climate in Ohio was so dismally poor as to be virtually nonexistent, such that any opportunities I had to find worthwhile employment suited to my skills and abilities, or to start up a new business (and convince a bank to provide me with the capital to do so) were equally nonexistent, assuming the parole board would even think about allowing me to embark on a new business enterprise, which in and of itself was highly unlikely. If business and industry was on life support in Ohio, it at least had a pulse back in Alaska.

After having miscalculated, rather prodigiously, about all of these situations, what else could I have possibly misjudged or failed to apprehend about this brilliant plan of mine to come back "home" to the Buckeye State?

The answer to that question was massively ironic, and it was enormously psychologically and spiritually disturbing to me as well. From the moment I said my goodbyes to my friends in Alaska, before I stepped onto the plane that brought me here, I began to miss all of those people dearly. I had a church that I could go to and feel welcome and accepted for what I was, where I felt like no one there was judging me. Pastor Tom was very supportive and very good to me, even though he openly and bluntly told me—much to my astonishment—that he did not approve of my lifestyle, and actually warned me that if I did not reform my ways, my soul would never attain everlasting life! Well, he was a good man—still is—but I guess no one is perfect! In the end, honestly, I could only be mildly amused at Pastor Tom's spiritual myopia, and hell, at least it meant that *someone else* was concerned for the welfare of my soul besides me! But in truth, the angry side of me, and the side of me that knew that I had always tried to do the right thing in all of my personal and business dealings, felt like confronting him by saying, "Never mind about my 'redemption' in everlasting life; how about getting some tiny measure of redemption in *this life*?!" But, of course, I would never do such a thing.

And there was DJ, a female member of the congregation with whom I carried on a long-distance regular correspondence by letter and also talked to regularly on the phone. DJ was divorced, and she and I had become close friends shortly after I joined Pastor Tom's church. However, I think that DJ wanted more, and I believe that she hoped to "convert" me as well. That certainly wasn't going to happen, but just like with Pastor Tom, I felt good about the fact that clearly DJ cared a lot about me as well. In Ashland there is a church on just about every street corner (and a liquor store on the opposite corner), yet during the two years I would spend on parole in Ohio, I was never able to find a congregation where I felt welcome and accepted for what I am, or where I felt I wasn't being gossiped about behind my back.

I missed Jim Lewis very much, too. Sure, he was an inveterate alcoholic who just couldn't seem to stop drinking and getting himself into trouble with the law time and time again, and as a result, a regular overnight guest at the Anchorage jail, but I missed our rigorous hikes through those magnificent forested mountains punctuated with lakes and streams. Despite PO Bleucher's strict prohibitions, I talked regularly by phone with Jim and a host of other ex-cons back home in Alaska, many of whom, I now realized, had become my best friends even if they sometimes did try to mooch some money off me. In my journal when I made note of these conversations, I was careful not to refer to these friends by name so that Bleucher could not easily identify them as being on my "banned" list, though of course, because she had access to my telephone records on demand, I was aware that she was probably able to track down my contact with any of my fellow reprobates if she had a mind to. So I was taking a risk of sorts. But I desperately needed that contact. In so many of those conversations, with Pastor Tom or DJ, with Jim Lewis and the other guys I met when I was in Palmer Correctional, and even with Janet Dawson and some of the other corrections people—there were a number of them who were really decent people whom I liked very much and who treated me with some respect. All of these folks would ask the same question of me, over and over, whenever we talked on the phone: "When are you coming home?"

And when I reflected on all of this, all that I could think was, how could I have been so blind? The fact of the matter was that I had amassed a significant community of caring and concerned friends up there. I remember the first time it finally hit me, when I said to myself, "Holy shit!"—when I realized I had actually created a 'life after prison' for myself in Alaska! It wasn't exactly the life I would have planned, and there were still some significant holes in it: in particular, I had not managed to find gainful employment, or what would have been even better, to get back into some sort of new business venture or enterprise, which is really my true passion, but it wasn't for want of trying. In hindsight, I could speculate that perhaps I hadn't given that effort, of building a new life in my adoptive state, enough time, and that perhaps I had wasted some valuable emotional and motivational energy obsessing about returning to my ancestral home— energy that I could have focused on starting a new business against all the odds, or at least, on connecting with a somewhat different community that the one I had known previously. A rationalization, maybe, but the truth of the matter is that I came out of prison with a singular, monolithic, and admittedly myopic resolve to "go home," and I would have to concede that it might not have been the right thing to do after all.

Moreover, the life that I had built there, and which seemed also to have developed largely by itself, all around me without my really being consciously aware of it, was still evolving. It was something like John Lennon famously observed, though I believe he may have taken it from somewhere else: "Life is what happens when you're making other plans." But in truth, I had actually been very busy helping out with activities and functions at my church; I had enjoyed leisure time again thanks to those long hikes through the mountains with Jim, which were also extremely good for both my physical and mental, psychological health. One evening in Ashland in September of 2010, I sat down to write my last journal entry for the day, a day in which I had long, enjoyable conversations with both Janet Dawson and Jim Lewis back in Anchorage. Almost unconsciously, I wrote, "I am missing Alaska; there was *so much more* to do there!"—emphasis added. I was less than two months back home in Ohio at this time. I stared at the line I had written. It was a crystallizing moment. And apparently, Alaska was missing me, too.

Remarkably, I had had a rich and varied life going on there after all, and somehow, unwittingly, I had left it behind! Like the Joni Mitchell song says: "You don't know what you've got til it's gone."

If all of this sounds like a beautiful, inspiring, eye-opening revelation and, maybe even the portal to a happy ending of the Disney movie version of my life, it was by no means whatsoever a wondrous and welcome nirvana to me—not by a long shot. Because, as I had realized, no matter what the courts and the lawyers and the DOC and parole boards had done to destroy my life, I had managed to find a way to dig an even deeper hole for myself by, at a minimum, not exactly thinking through very carefully the decision that landed me back in Ashland. Worse, as time passed, I was losing touch with all of those folks who had become, almost without my realizing it, my best friends and associates and extremely important to me in my life. That part of the realization only served to heighten my anxiety and my agitated sense of urgency to get back to Alaska before it was too late, before I lost contact with those people entirely and forever. But as I stated it earlier, I was trapped. I had enmeshed myself back into a world that I had broken free of two decades earlier, and getting free of it a second time wasn't going to be so easy. In fact, I would live with this intolerable situation for a full three years before it was me that finally broke.

A Night on the Town

I am not a big drinker, but having said that, let me qualify that statement. I love good food; I love great restaurants that serve exquisite dishes, and at home I'm a pretty darn good cook myself. And an important component of the great dining experience is the fine wine that one pairs with the meal, and I'd have to say I have an appreciation for an impeccable Bordeaux or a great California chardonnay—in short, I know my way around a well-stocked wine shop. But I have never been a hard-drinking bar-hopper, even in my youth when going to bars was about the only thing one could do to meet people, or to have a good time, or so my friends and I thought when we were really still just kids. That was until one night, now in my 50s and back living in Ohio after some 20 years away from the place, one night when I felt utter despair and hopelessness over my predicament, and felt as though I was at the end of my rope. I said to myself, "Fuck everything!" and I got in the car and drove off to Columbus to hit the bars and just "go drinking" for the hell of it. Isn't that what people do when they're depressed; go out and drink to have a good time? It was a warm evening in late July of 2011, and I guess you could call it my somewhat cynical celebration of my one-year anniversary of being back in Ohio.

It wasn't precisely that I intended to commit suicide via drunk driving. I'd tried suicide a couple of times before and I proved to be a failure at even doing that. No, it was more that I just didn't care anymore about what might happen. I felt—I had long felt by this time—that my life was in a state of ruin that was irreparable, that the only thing left for me to lose was life itself. And this life I was now reduced to was in reality no life at all. So losing it in a fiery car crash would actually mean losing nothing at all, except of course the car. But of course, you can't drive when you're dead anyway, so what the hell? So I drove off that evening to get deliberately, recklessly drunk, and with any luck, killed in Columbus in a blaze of glory. But instead of going out in a spectacular and apocalyptic explosion of flame and twisted steel, I ran over a huge rock which ripped off the oil pan. Undeterred in my quest for oblivion, I continued to drive madly down the road; that is, until all the oil ran out and the engine seized, and my drunken joy ride was over. I was promptly arrested and charged with DUI, as well as a few of the customary lesser "throw away" charges that police officers like to write in such instances. Actually, I was turned in by my own car, which had all of the state-of-the-art electronics built into it, including the driver assistance software, so as soon as I hit the rock, the car automatically called emergency services—and notified the police! Even my own car had turned against me! So much for the benefits of modern digital communications technology! In any case, I was hauled off to the Columbus jail, where I spent three days until my Aunt and Uncle came to pick me up and take me home. When I signed out for my personal possessions and they handed me the large manila envelope, it was missing my ring and over $200 from my wallet. When I protested to the desk sergeant that the ring and money were missing, he glibly replied that I could file a complaint if I wanted to. I didn't bother, as it was immediately apparent to me that it would be a fight that I could not win. Besides, I already had enough of dealing with law enforcement on my hands.

The reaction to my automotive adventure from my parole officer was swift and, I have to admit, pin-pointedly decisive. She ordered me to appear in her office on August 4th, the first day after I got out of Columbus jail. I fully expected that this incident would constitute a sufficiently serious offense—it certainly must have involved multiple parole violations—to compel PO Bleucher to give me a "fail" on my parole and send me back to Palmer Correctional to finish out the rest of my sentence in prison. In fact, I expressly asked her to send me back, telling her there was simply nothing for me, and nothing that I was allowed to do, in Ohio. I honestly wanted to go back to Palmer and just flat-time the rest of my sentence, and get it all over with. She refused. Why, I don't know, but I suspect that in her own perverse way, PO Bleucher was bound and determined to reform me, although she claimed that she had conferred with DOC officials in Alaska who instructed her about what to do with me. I should have told her to take a number and get in line. She ordered me to submit to 60 days of electronic monitoring, which would be conducted by a company with the unlikely name of Voice of America, or VOA for short. For my part, I retained a very good attorney and DUI defense specialist in Columbus to handle my case. The hearing was scheduled for August 30th at 9:00 am. I wondered if there would be anything said in court about my missing money and ring: somehow, I doubted that there would be.

 The electronic monitoring by VOA was both a joke and a nightmare all rolled into one. These utterly incompetent people called me on the phone incessantly, sometimes 15 or 20 times a day, to tell me—to threaten me, actually—that they weren't getting a signal and demanding to know where I was. And I was right there at home. In the days and weeks after the accident I was virtually *always* at home. There was no purposeful place for me to go, and nothing for me to do, plus there was no way for me to get there, since my car was a wreck being evaluated by the mechanics at the dealership. The plain fact was that I had absolutely no desire to go out anyway, preferring to stay home because it was the only place where I felt safe, and where I believed I couldn't be accused of doing anything wrong or of getting into more trouble. But VOA was relentless and merciless: they called me at all hours of the night always saying the same thing: they were not getting a signal and they wanted to know where I was. As if I didn't already have enough trouble getting a decent night's sleep with all of the depression and anxiety I was feeling. On at least one occasion, they called at about 2:00 am, and they actually wanted me to walk outside the house into the middle of a raging thunderstorm—lightning, thunder, monsoon rains; the works—so that they could try to pick up the signal from the monitor I had to wear. I imagined that I would not get another uninterrupted night's sleep until October, when this idiotic 60-day monitoring would finally be over. It was as pathetic as it was infuriating and frustrating.

I was spiraling deeper and deeper, and dangerously, into myself and shutting out everybody and everything more severely than ever. When my insurance representative called to tell me that the damage to the car was so bad that he wanted to total it out, I said, "Good!" There was no place left for me to go anyway, and no place I wanted to go: Who needs a car? I'd save money on gas and maintenance, on the car wash; hell, I'd save money on insurance and registration fees—why was I paying for all of that stuff anyway? At right about this same time I decided to cancel my cell phone—why pay for that when I didn't have any worthwhile business to conduct? Nor at this point, did I want to talk to any living person whatsoever!

My DUI attorney did not receive the discovery for my case from the prosecutor's office until the Friday before the hearing, which gave us only the following Monday to discuss my defense. That, of course is calculated—the state certainly doesn't want to give you a lot of time to plan a compelling and powerful opposing argument through which you might actually be able to refute the charges. Not that it mattered, because on the trial date the case was almost instantly postponed until October 6th. No surprise to me: through all of my vast and still burgeoning experience in both civil and criminal court, I had witnessed so many postponements and attorney's motions for re-scheduled hearings that I was beginning to think that there was some sort of law on the books that mandated that no court case proceeding was allowed to be conducted without at least one—and preferably multiple—postponements and re-schedulings. So, as I was so used to doing, I went home to wait for the next hearing. Nothing new in the U.S. court system.

In the meantime, PO Bleucher wasn't quite yet through with me over this incident either, or with her noble quest to rehabilitate me. Because in a meeting about a week later she ordered me to make an appointment with the Appleseed Community Mental Health Center in Ashland, and to make arrangements to see a counsellor there on a regular and ongoing basis. PO Bleucher said that this psychiatric and psychological counseling was for the benefit of my "mental health." However, I can sum up the full net value of my Appleseed mental health counselling program in one sentence. They said, in essence:

"You're not insane or suicidal, Jerry, you're just depressed."

I received the dubious benefit of this lightning bolt of a diagnosis through countless wasted hours "on the couch," metaphorically speaking, with my psychological therapist, and I'm sure that Sigmund Freud and Carl Jung would be just so proud of them!

In any event, on the newly appointed day for the hearing in October, my case finally got before the judge. One of the things

I was ordered to do was to participate in a class called "Second Chance Counselling," a 3-day, overnight affair that was to be conducted in early November in the town of Delaware, Ohio at, of all places, the Comfort Inn. Over these three days of classes, a series of instructors taught my classmates and me about the perils of alcohol and drug abuse, and the even greater dangers of driving while drinking or drugging, but the only thing I remember about it was that when they put us into our hotel rooms for the night, their security technology consisted of putting masking tape across all of the door jambs—if the tape was broken in the morning, you had been effectively caught "red-handed" breaking curfew. We all thought this was pretty hysterical, and well, I really needed a good laugh at that particular time. It was just another classroom-style remedial program in a state where they seemed so fond of them that I started to think: Maybe for my next business venture I should come up with some sort of rehabilitation organization designed to help people who, for whatever reason imaginable, might have run afoul of the laws of the state—by all accounts there certainly was an ample supply of them! Line up a few contracts with the DOC, and I'd be living the high life again! My case was then continued to December 19th to give me time to comply with the judge's order to attend "Second Chance Counseling."

Since it was my first DUI conviction, in the final hearing in December, the judge sentenced me to 90 days in jail, but said the sentence would be suspended if I attended the 3-day Second Chance Counseling session, which of course I had done. He also hit me with a monetary fine and ordered a year of supervised probation, but he did not revoke my driving privileges at all. I've said some unkind things about attorneys throughout this book, but I have to say, based on the light sentence I received in my DUI case, my attorney from Columbus had done a very good job in representing me this time around. The irony was that, when you tallied up all of the ramifications resulting from this incident, PO Bleucher put more stuff on me, what with the electronic monitoring and the psychological counseling, than the judge did. So, in the end, my personal legal status had hardly changed as a result of my drunken escapade and resulting car crash. I was already on probation as it was, and I still had my driver's license, though I no longer had a nice car to drive. The psychological status of my emotional and mental health, however, was a few notches lower.

CHAPTER 7
MY BOOK: BANNED IN OHIO

A Reason for Being

Throughout all of this adversity, there was one thing that kept me going, if only to a limited extent. From the time I got out of prison in Alaska, I was determined to write a book about my life, and shortly after my release, I began working with an editor on a manuscript. It was something of a struggle. Not that it was particularly difficult; in fact, the first several chapters, which became a straightforward narrative covering my upbringing and teenage years through my earliest business ventures and up to my migration to Alaska, were relatively easy to write. We all have, I imagine, relatively vivid memories of our youth and of growing up. However, I would submit that growing up gay in Ashland, Ohio during the 1960s and 70s is not something that one easily forgets.

Nevertheless, for a very long time my work on the book was very slow going, even with the assistance of my editor. For one thing, there were just so many distractions, what with dealing with the DOC and my parole officers or the sheriff's office; trying to get back into some sort of business venture again; or worst of all, having to process the reams of paperwork in connection with my lawsuit against my former partner and I-Care Pharmacy in Maine, along with seemingly endless consultations with my attorneys on the case. I guess I'd also have to concede that through those times when my depression was at its worst, I simply lost interest in writing the book just as I periodically lost interest in everything else—those times when life itself felt so utterly meaningless that I would find myself asking, "Why bother?" So writing my first book became an on-again off-again affair, and the manuscript was less than half finished a year later when I flew home to Ohio in late July of 2010.

Maybe it was the resounding, mind-numbing boredom of my "new life" in Ashland County, or the severity of the restrictions and the reporting requirements of my new DOC overlords, or even as an escape from my combative and endlessly feuding parents, but within a few months of my return, I renewed my commitment, not just to getting the book written, but also to getting it published. As I mentioned in Chapter 4, it quickly became clear to me that writing my book was perhaps the only constructive thing I would be able do while I was still "on paper" with the overbearingly restrictive Ohio parole system. And as I said, it felt downright subversive to be writing it, because the parole board and PO Bleucher absolutely did not approve, having actually warned me against writing it, and there is no doubt in my mind that they would have prevented me from writing it if there was any legal means though which they could stop me. If it felt a little subversive or rebellious for me to be writing what I hoped would become something of an exposé of the legal system—both of the judicial branch and of the Department of Corrections—well, that was one of the few pleasurable pursuits that I had going on during those dark days while I was on paper. And in fact, it did give me something constructive within which to immerse myself, either when I was bored or when mom and dad were re-enacting famous battles from World War II. What's more, finally, writing the book was something I could do within the confines of my own home; I didn't need to go anywhere to do it, and I didn't need anyone's permission to work on it.

Fortunately, only a few months after returning to Ashland, I was referred to a new editor to help me with the book project, and we began in earnest just after Thanksgiving. It would continue to be a slow process that would take almost another year to complete, but progress this time around was more methodical and was more focused on a definitive and tangible end-goal of formal publication—and promotion—of the book.

As I said earlier, the easier part of my story had already been pretty much written. And indeed, I wanted to talk about my life growing up, the first small businesses I started and ran successfully, the lessons I learned from the more significant business mistakes I made along the way, and how I transformed them into tremendous success later on. I wanted to talk about the circumstances that led me to set out on my own for a new "frontier" in Alaska, and in particular, I wanted to talk about my enormous success in the health care and pharmaceutical industries in Alaska and later in Maine, as well as the big plans I had to expand my companies to provide even more varied and better health care services to hundreds of thousands of people in those two states, and perhaps beyond them someday. If I might be permitted to say so, I thought I had done pretty well in business, in starting one company from scratch, rescuing another from bankruptcy and corruption, and turning both of them into multi-million dollar organizations in very short periods of time. And not simply done well for myself, but for all of people who were my employees and customers.

But that was not the intended primary focus of the book. To begin with, I resolved to talk candidly about the colossal mistake I made in my personal life which landed me in criminal court, and more significantly and importantly, which would eventually bring all of that good, highly beneficial work in the health care industry crashing down. With that said, what I really wanted to talk about in the book was to expose the failure of the justice system to ensure that I received a fair trial before a truly impartial jury of my peers. The full factual details underlying this failure are presented in my first book, *Derailed*, but for my purposes here, it is sufficient to say that the court's failure began with its obstinate, and I would say egotistical, selfish refusal to grant a simple and relatively harmless request for a change of venue to a district where I would have had the opportunity to present myself, and my case, before an impartial and unbiased jury. After that fateful, unyielding, and decidedly anti-egalitarian decision, things simply spiraled out of control, culminating in my being forced to cop a plea to a crime I did not commit, on advice of counsel who said basically, "Your guilt or innocence is irrelevant; you're not going to get a fair trial, therefore you're going to be convicted, and you have no other choice."

And in part, I wanted to show how this failure of the judicial system had such a profoundly destructive impact, not just on me personally, but on all of the people who were served by, and relied on, my healthcare and pharmaceutical companies. What must be understood is that the ramifications of the court's arrogance and stubbornness ultimately went far beyond sending one highly successful businessman to prison, who also happened to be gay (a combination that wasn't supposed to be able to happen in the Christian conservative community of the Wasilla Valley). Once those companies were destroyed, those people had no one else to turn to for their medical and healthcare needs. And all of that could have been avoided, if only I had been granted a fair hearing to present my case, as is supposed to be my right under the Constitution. Instead, a judge's ego, and a prosecutor more eager to rack up another conviction that to see justice served, ruled the day. In my view, the people lost.

Writing about these aspects, the true crux and purpose of that book, proved to be a more intense and complicated process, and I worked on it in a measured and more calculated fashion for the better part of 2011. By the end of the year, the book was ready to go to press!

I signed an agreement with a publisher to do the book in hardcover, paperback, and ebook formats, but I made what would turn out to be an even more valuable and crucial connection with Steve Harrison, a top publicist and media expert, whose company, Bradley Communications, is based in the Philadelphia area, and which has particularly strong connections with radio and TV networks across the entire U.S. This guy really delivered. Because it seemed that, no sooner was *Derailed* officially published on December 15th, 2011, I almost instantly started getting calls to do interviews on radio stations across the country from New York to California; though in hindsight, I realize that's a bit of an exaggeration on my part. In actuality, it took a couple of months for things to really start happening and for the buzz about the book to start hitting the airwaves. After all, my publisher's marketing campaign did not kick off until the very end of February into the month of March, after several months of hard work collaborating with the people in the promotions and publicity departments there. Also, Bradley Communications' primary publicity tool is the magazine called "Radio and TV Interview Report" (RTIR), which is published quarterly, and thus the first opportunity to promote *Derailed* in print was in the March 1, 2012 issue. But I guess I could say that I was more buoyant in my attitude, more optimistic about my prospects for something positive in my future, and I was even getting a little bit excited about life again with the publication of the book. I even went and bought a new car in February (which I had to do online with a dealership in Columbus, because there was no place in Ashland where I could arrange a decent deal), after I had sworn, right after my accident, that I didn't want or need one anymore!

Even further, I started making auspicious plans to write a second book. I wanted to write about the flaws that I perceived—and still perceive—in our nation's courts, in our correctional system, and more broadly, in our justice system as a whole. In particular I wanted to write more broadly about the serious erosion of constitutional rights that I see happening in this country, a continuing situation that I am extremely concerned about. I began researching and compiling relevant published scholarly-academic documents and information from the internet and the public library, and I sent copies of it all to my editor, asking for his help with the conceptual development, and in particular, to help me sharply define the thematic content and scope that the new book should have. I believe, along with many other people, there is a great deal wrong with our system of justice; that it has become corrupted and runs rough-shod over the constitutional rights of citizens—both prior to and after trial—and there would be a lot of factual data to cover. But what was most vital to me, I believe, was that I was beginning to grow some enthusiasm for doing something that I believed would be very important and useful for me to do, and which could help people; though in a way that was somewhat different from the way I had helped them through my health care companies. I still believe that fixing the U.S. justice system, and in particular, restoring the preeminence of the basic rights and individual freedoms that are supposed to be embodied in our Constitution, represent one of the most critical challenges that American citizens face in the modern 21st century.

In any case, the buzz surrounding *Derailed* actually began to build even before the publisher fully launched their marketing campaign and before the book was featured in the March edition of RTIR. I believe that was due in large part to the fact that as early as November and all through December and January I was furiously writing letters to anybody I could think of who might be interested in the book, whether they might like and appreciate the fact that I wrote and published it—or might hate the very idea and might be really worried or upset about what I had to say in its pages. In a pique of bemusement, I thought about writing to some good friends of mine who also happened to be the owners of Mad Myrna's and O'Brady's Burger and Brew, both gay bars in Anchorage that I used to frequent from time to time. In fact, O'Brady's was a Scottish-Irish style pub from which I got some of the ideas I used when I designed The Irish Setter Pub in Presque Isle, Maine. But I decided against it. It had been a long, long time since I had seen them, and I thought that, well, maybe that just wasn't appropriate. Some days I sent out 40 or more letters to friends and associates.

And of course, I wrote a letter to Jane Battier up in Maine about the book's publication. Jane had been one of the few people, perhaps the only person other than my family, who had given me such enormous and uncompromising moral support throughout the whole ordeal from my arrest, through the trial and the plea deal, and as no other except for my parents, she helped to keep me sane throughout the 16 months I sat incarcerated in Palmer correctional, with her wacky letters and jokes. And besides, Jane figured prominently in the story of *Derailed*—under a pseudonym of course—so I was sure she would want to read all about herself!

One night on the telephone, after she had read the book, Jane had me in stitches.

"I can recognize who I am in there, you know," she said.

"Well I should hope so," I laughed. Then she told me that she bought an extra copy to give to my ex-lover and former business partner, with whom I had just concluded, in October of 2011, an ugly and downright vicious lawsuit (though the fallout and ramifications of that lawsuit and its so-called "settlement" still continue to this day).

"Did you really give him a copy?" I asked incredulously.

"Of course," she replied. "He should read it too, you know!"

I laughed until there were tears in my eyes!

In early December, just days before the book came out, I contacted the ACLU of Ohio and the Ohio Aids Coalition and I offered to donate some of the proceeds of the sales to those organizations, provided of course the book sold well enough to generate any significant royalties. In truth, I wasn't looking to get rich off of *Derailed*; what I truly wanted was to make known this injustice that had happened to me in the courts and to shine a light on the fact that it goes on all the time, to all kinds of people, right up to this day. In any event, I have to say I was surprised—but delighted—to find some copies of *Derailed* on the shelf at the local Barnes and Noble bookstore on December16[th], just one day after it's "official" publication. Through the end of 2011 and into January of the New Year, I continued to work closely with my publisher and with Bradley Communications on their respective marketing and promotions campaigns for my first-ever published book. My publisher set up a number of book signing events at various local bookstores in Columbus, Mansfield, and elsewhere through January and February, and we were off and running!

Let the Buzz Begin!

Things were relatively quiet through January, but then on February 5th, the Anchorage Daily News published some excerpts from *Derailed* in its Saturday edition. It was only a very small piece, and it is purely conjecture on my part, but I wonder if it was those excerpts in the paper which got the attention of DOC officials in Alaska. Of course, the guards and corrections officials might have just as easily found out about the book from any of my good friends inside Palmer Correctional. Inmates, for all their general lack of education, are notoriously avid book and newspaper readers, and sometimes there can even be a kind of pecking-order battle when there are only a limited number of copies of the morning edition available. After all, what else is there to do in there but fight over the morning paper? Anyway, I suspect that the Alaska DOC officials no doubt relayed their concerns to their colleagues in Ohio, although I had made no attempt at all to hide the fact that I had written and published it—quite the contrary, I was telling everybody I could about it. But apparently, they were none too pleased with any of this publicity, or the book, or... especially... with me. So it wasn't too long, about 10 days later, that PO Bleucher paid one of her unannounced visits to my parents' home. Bleucher told me that she had heard about the book (quelle surprise!), and said she was interested in reading it. She seemed pretty coy about it. So I thought I'd be coy in return.

"Well," I said, "It's at the Barnes and Noble; you can buy a copy." However, she informed me that the DOC had no budget for buying books or anything else produced by parolees. I said, "Well here, I'll give you a copy; with my compliments," and I held a copy out for her to take.

She shook her head. "We're not allowed to take any gifts from parolees either," she said, and I waited for her to tell me what she had in mind.

"I'm only allowed to borrow a copy," she said, "And then I'm required to return it." She took the paperback copy and left. My next appointment with her was scheduled for March 7th, and it was a doozy.

PO Bleucher informed me that I was prohibited from doing any radio or TV interviews in connection with promoting or even talking about my book. I was not allowed to do any book signing engagements, nor was I permitted to travel for any purpose relating to promoting *Derailed*. It turned out that Bleucher hadn't read my book; in fact, she had absolutely no interest at all in reading it at all, not that I was particularly surprised at this. Instead, she had gotten the book solely in order to pass it up the chain of command to her superiors at DOC headquarters in Columbus so that they could come down with their inevitable ruling that *Derailed* should be banned and I must be silenced. PO Bleucher undoubtedly thought she had been pretty clever in the way that she managed to "borrow" a copy of the book on the pretext of wanting to read it, but then surreptitiously sending it up to High Command, when in fact I would have been more than happy to offer a very attractive discount in return for a bulk sale so that everyone in the DOC could get a copy to read!

More seriously, though, here was the Ohio Department of Rehabilitation and Corrections telling me to stop promoting or even talking about my book, and specifically ordering me to cease doing any more book signings or radio interviews. Bleucher told me that the order came directly from the Department's headquarters in Columbus, and predictably, of course, she claimed she had nothing to do with the decision, which even she conceded seemed to be pretty harsh. Whether Bleucher was being sincere or not, I believe that her obvious desire to distance herself from this order was a clear indication, at the very least, that she recognized this was just plain wrong on the part of DOC. Nevertheless, she said to me quite pointedly, "Don't even attempt to request a travel pass for the purpose of doing a book signing, or an interview, or anything else for promoting the book, because it will not be approved." No ifs, ands, or buts.

My mind was reeling, and I was sick to my stomach. I don't think I was fully able to process this information immediately. Surely we were talking about my First Amendment right to free speech here, weren't we? Certainly, Bleucher and the DOC weren't suggesting that they were going to take away from me one of the most fundamental, cornerstone rights upon which our democratic nation was founded, were they? I left the meeting, I have to say, speechless and rather confused, because I don't think that I could actually believe, or even assimilate, what I had just been told. At first it just didn't seem to register, but the import of what I had been told lingered in the back of my mind like the proverbial bad dream, and my anger swelled over the next several days, but even then I don't think I was prepared to take it seriously, at least not yet. It was just so unbelievable as to be inconceivable: Who in America would tolerate the suspension of their freedom of speech? It seemed that I would have to take Bleucher's prohibitions seriously, but I would refuse to abide by them to whatever extent I could resist. When I was able to collect myself a few days later, I wrote letters about this outrage to the ACLU and to the attorney in Columbus who had done such a fine job handling my DUI case several months earlier.

Events accelerated nevertheless. On March 12th I did an interview with a radio station at 1240 on the AM dial out of Maryland. On March 18th, a pre-recorded interview for a show called "Indie Book Publishing" and hosted by Steve Jorgenson for something called TogiNet Radio, out of Loma Linda, aired in Southern California, including the coverage area of Los Angeles. Of course, with today's digital streaming audio, even these locally based radio stations could conceivably have listeners across the country, or around the world for that matter. (The Indie Book Publishing interview with Steve Jorgenson, for example, is still listener-accessible in the Archive bank on TogiNet's website.) I did another radio interview on April 3rd on KCAA AM, also out of California, but an important NBC affiliate. All the while of course, in the back of my mind I wondered what the fallout from ignoring PO Bleucher's prohibitions and doing all these interviews in rapid-fire succession was going to be. The book signing appearances were out; I could no longer do them because she would refuse to approve any travel out of Ashland county for that purpose, but I was determined that I would continue any radio or other media interviews that could be conducted by telephone—out of the privacy of my own home—and thus would not require me to travel.

Both the ACLU and my Columbus attorney came back with the same unsatisfactory and unnerving legal opinion. No, they said, the parole board had absolutely no right to suspend or prohibit my First Amendment freedom of speech, but yes, they could do whatever that wanted to do with me and get away with it. The ACLU said basically that they could not help me and politely declined to get involved. My attorney was even more blunt. He said, in essence, "Sure, we can take them to court, and the case will take a year, maybe two to prosecute, and it will cost you an enormous amount of money. And by then of course, your book will be completely forgotten about, so even if you win the case, you lose the war." I appreciated his candor, even as I seethed with anger over a system that I already knew was broken and unjust, and stacked against me. This was, in part at least, the kind of gross misuse of governmental power and control, and the usurpation of individual, constitutional rights, that I wanted to make the subject of my next book.

"You're at their mercy," my attorney said, which was really just another way of saying what corrections and parole officers in both Alaska and Ohio had told me, both obliquely and in several instances, with eye-popping, diabolical directness without equivocation: "You have no rights whatsoever except those which we decide to give you." And in fact, the whole issue might never make it to court. If I were to fight against this intolerable usurpation of my constitutional rights, all the parole board would have to do would be to trump up some parole violation against me and send me back to prison. Fact was, I'd already given them plenty of ammo for doing that. As I've tried to stress throughout this book, it is all about control. Not only that, but the loose and arbitrary enforcement of the so-called "conditions of parole" means that, not only do the DOC and the parole board demand to have complete control over parolees, they also define what control itself actually means—and that, of course, varies widely according to their whim. If control requires them to trample on a citizen's constitutional rights, so be it. I, for one, find this incredible, unconscionable, and utterly unacceptable in America. I wasn't entirely sure what I was going to do, but I did know that I wasn't going to roll over so easily on an issue so fundamental to my country's core beliefs as the freedom of speech, not to mention the rights to privacy and of association.

Then two days after the KCAA interview aired, I got the most intriguing, exciting, and in some ways, the most seductive offer of all. I received an email from a fellow by the name of Brad Saul who introduced himself as the President of a 32 year old radio/syndication satellite network, based in Chicago, with 57 shows airing, in combination, on about 1,000 affiliate radio stations across the country. Brad also stated that his company, Matrix Media, had successfully launched The NBA Radio Network, The Sears College Football Game of The Week, Kudlow and Cramer on Radio, Animal Planet Radio, and Pet News to what he termed "terrestrial radio," which I gather is the new term to describe land-based radio in the new age of satellite communications and internet streaming.

In his email, Brad went on to explain what he believed was an important trend in radio, writing in part, "There has been a change in media over the past couple of years, led by Rosie O'Donnell, Ellen Degenerous (sic), and Rachel Madow (sic), [in] finding media personalities [who] are comfortable enough to not hide behind their sexuality and host radio and television programs." Brad went on to say that, up to that time, there had "not been a man who has hosted a talk radio program and is gay."

I found this pretty remarkable, if true, and yet for the life of me, I could not in fact think of a male radio talk show host who was openly gay, though of course I was admittedly only familiar with the well-known and ubiquitous media celebrities like shock-jocks Stern and Imus.

In his email and in subsequent conversations, Brad made it clear that he was not looking necessarily for someone simply for the sake of being gay, nor to talk exclusively about the issues that face lesbians and gays as they deal in the world of business. But at the same time, he indicated that, as a matter of course, LGBT issues may well be part of the discussion in any given episode of the talk radio program that the individual personality may host. Further, Brad said that he was looking specifically for a candidate who, in addition to being gay, must understand the world of business, the difficult global economic times in which we live, and the way the world is evolving into an entirely new paradigm. Finally, he stressed that this was a paying position, and that his network was not a "pay for play" service. I figured the pay would certainly not be substantial, but regardless, it would be nice to be working and doing something productive finally, and making a few dollars in the endeavor, especially if it gave me a way to help people again.

Well, all of this sat perfectly fine with me. For one thing, I had no particular desire to be some sort of champion or trailblazer for the LGBT community, nice though that might be. I am really a private person, and I had learned, out of some necessity, to become even more of a private person throughout the ordeal of prison and now being on paper, where everything I did was scrutinized unceasingly by the state. Moreover, the issues I wanted to talk about were clearly far broader than simply the issues of gay rights or discrimination in the workplace, or even such discrimination in society at large. It is vitally important to understand that the injustice that I was subjected to, and which I argue pervades our country's court systems, and the equally unjust correctional and parole system, which is deliberately and inherently designed to *keep people in* the system rather than to *encourage them to get out* of it to become productive members of society, are directed against *all of the people, regardless of race, creed, sexual orientation, or anything else*. In other words, this is not just about gay rights; what I am talking about in this book affects everyone who calls him or herself a citizen of this country—or wants to become one—and it is about the gradual but relentless erosion of our fundamental constitutional rights and freedoms.

Finally, I had an abundance of the kind of business experience and an acute understanding of the deplorable state of the business climate in this country in the new millennium, which did not come solely from having built Immediate Care in Alaska and I-Care Pharmacy in Maine into highly successful $30 million dollar companies. Because over the more than two and a half years since

I was released from prison, in researching dozens if not hundreds of promising and not-so-promising business opportunities across dozens of states in the U.S., I had learned about or experienced first-hand the tangled morass of bureaucratic red tape, as well as the onerous government and environmental regulations that are choking American business and free enterprise in the 21st Century. And I would have a lot to say about that, too, as a radio talk show host on Brad Saul's network.

Brad asked me if I was interested, and I was absolutely all in. I signed a contract on April 11th, knowing full-well that this was probably going to create a firestorm of difficulty for me over at the Department of Corrections. I was slated to host my first broadcast radio interview show on May 14th.

Throughout all of our discussions, I was completely candid and up-from with Brad about my situation at that particular time. He assured me that they could set up everything so that I could conduct the show from my home—I wouldn't have to travel anywhere, and therefore I wouldn't be faced with trying to obtain permission to do so. I might have to do some major updates on my computer, but I was perfectly willing to buy the equipment to do so on my own dime. (I did figure I'd probably have to buy a good, secure lock for the door in order to keep my perpetually arguing parents out of the room with the computer while I recorded the show!) I'd have a paying gig on a radio program broadcast from the private confines of my home, over the telephone, away from any places that the state said I shouldn't be, and while on-air, at least, they could always know exactly where I was, and so I reasoned—quite cynically of course—what possible objection could the Ohio DOC have to that?

Lots, it would turn out.

Ultimately, I disregarded PO Bleucher's order to cease doing interviews and talking about my book, or what had become my life's story over the past several years. I must have done a dozen or more interviews for AM radio stations across the country, all or most of which were also broadcast over satellite or the internet; so many in fact, that I cannot remember all the stations or the call letters for most of them. I appeared on stations with liberal-minded leanings and audience demographics, but I was also invited to talk on those with a more conservative viewpoint, of which a station in Denver stands out in my mind because, despite their conservatism, I thought they treated me quite well and allowed me to air my views without chastising, denigrating, or even disrespecting them in any way. As I stated earlier in this chapter, the issues I wanted to raise, both with my book and in my speaking appearances, affect all people—conservatives as well as liberals, people of all races and sexual orientations, and so on. The last interview I would get to do was with Ronald Zack of Arizona Law Review Radio—a conservative "red" state certainly—and yet Ron was good enough to explore objectively the circumstances surrounding my court case that compelled my own attorneys to advise me to take the plea deal rather than fight the charges, which was my legal right.

Unfortunately, however, the Ohio DOC did manage to quash what would have been that first show as a radio host, on the 14th of May, on the Matrix Media network. Brad Saul's organization could not afford to take the risk of violating a direct order from the State of Ohio. For Brad's sake I had to understand; after all, he had been tremendously supportive of me all along the way, and of what I was trying to do, as he is to this day. As for the state of Ohio, I felt that they had really stuck it to me this time. For nearly three years I had struggled to find something productive in business or industry that I could do to "get back in the entrepreneurial game," as my Air Force uncle had put it when I first got out of prison. But the DOCs in two states had stopped me at every turn. Now, finally, I had found something I could do that I believed would be productive and useful, even important, and which would not be at odds with anything that the state required of me in my current status as a parolee, and yet they had put an immediate stop to that as well. Not only that, but in practical terms, the radio program would have been an opportunity for me to start generating an income again, and to start digging out of the deepening financial hole I was in. Needless to say, I was devastated. It seemed that no matter what I tried, and no matter how honest I was about it, the state was never going to allow me to do anything to make my intolerable situation any better for myself, or my family. And they were devious, secretive, and underhanded about it, never providing me with any legal reasons for their "cease and desist" orders, but simply saying "no," and in effect, "tough shit."

The Game Comes to an End

The last thing I want to say about *Derailed* and my desire to promote and prosper from it is this: I would argue strongly that continuing to do these interviews wasn't precisely an act of direct defiance, or something I wanted to belligerently throw back in the face of the authorities who had jurisdiction over me just out of spite. I had been a model of compliance and "respect" for authority, from prison to parolee. The fact is, throughout all of the time I was on parole up to this point, I had not directly defied anything that the DOC authorities, parole boards and officers, or sheriff's offices had ordered or instructed me to do. I am by no means a defiant or arbitrary person by nature—in fact I think I am quite the opposite, someone who tries to get along with everyone and play by the rules, often to the fault of injuring myself rather than stand up and fight. Rather, I continued to talk about these issues out of principle, because I think I refused to accept the very concept that they had the right to in any way shut down my freedom of speech, and I clung to that apparently naïve belief. I wasn't going to sue them. No, let them just try to stop me. The rationale I used to neutralize my anxiety over what actions they might take was simply this: I was just talking on the phone, within the confines of my own home, and there's no law against that. There's no specific prohibitions against that in my "Conditions of Mandatory Parole." You could call them interviews if you wanted to, but from my perspective on things, I was just talking casually on the phone.

In any case, at this time I was also frequenting the casinos more often. Earlier in this book, I explained that the casinos had an enormous appeal to me because they were the only places where I felt like I didn't have to be constantly watching over my shoulder, where I was able to feel like an adult, and ultimately, just like everybody else in the room, where everyone was just trying to relax and have a good time. However, being available to do the radio shows from home meant that I was obliged to stick around the house more, which gave mom and dad more time to do their unsettling shenanigans, to get on my nerves, and cause me more aggravation and distress. Mom seemed to be drinking more than ever and at any time of the day, which meant more protracted, obnoxious phone calls with her sister and a host of others. Dad sat in his chair and did nothing but bark orders at me; sometimes he wouldn't so much get up and go the kitchen to get himself his own bowl of ice cream from the freezer. Why should he? All he had to do was yell to me and I'd go get it for him! And that may have been part of the reason I was going to the casinos so often. The interesting thing is that PO Bleucher kept giving me the travel passes pretty easily and without any remarks, or expressing any concerns or cautions about how often I was going. Perhaps she was feeling sorry for me over the whole book promotion refusal fiasco; maybe she was just giving me enough rope to hang myself; but whatever the reason, she just kept routinely issuing the passes without any comment.

On Friday, June 22, 2012, I got a travel pass to go to the casinos in Wheeling, West Virginia for the weekend. While I was there, it came to my attention that it was Gay Pride week, which is always a big, week-long celebration along the waterfront in Cleveland. So I decided to leave Wheeling and head up to the casinos in Cleveland instead. I did not have a travel pass for Cleveland, nor did I have permission to be there. And I probably would have gotten away with it, that is, until I decided to stay an extra day. Because when I did not return home on Sunday evening as scheduled, on Monday morning my mother called, of all people, Parole Officer Bleucher.

I do not know if my mother made this call "out of love and concern"; that is, out of such sincere care and concern for my welfare that when I did not return by Sunday evening, she was so worried that something serious might have happened to me that she didn't know who else to call or what else to do. This, of course, would have been the first instance I deeply regretted getting rid of my cell phone about a year earlier, or else she might have been able to call me instead of my official tormentor! Or alternatively—and just as plausible, sad to say—I don't know if she made the call because now for several days she had been without her little house boy to do the dishes and the laundry, to clean the house and mow the lawn, and all of the other chores my folks had saddled me with since I came home, while they sat around and did nothing but drink and argue. While I still loved her, I was so infuriated that I couldn't even bring myself to speak with her about what the hell she was thinking when she picked up that phone. So even to this day, I only know that, in jailhouse parlance, she had committed the most heinous of acts: she had ratted me out. My mother became a snitch.

In any event, I was summoned to a meeting with PO Bleucher two days later on Wednesday. I fully expected that I would not be coming back home from that meeting, but instead would be immediately whisked away and back to jail. However, that did not happen, nor did much of anything else, except to answer some pointed questions that she had. She ordered me to meet with her again on the morning of July 2nd, and I went home. When I showed up on the morning of the 2nd, she told me she was busy, and instructed me to come back at 1:30 in the afternoon. So infuriatingly typical. But virtually nothing happened at that meeting either, and I suspected that the state DOC was trying to figure out what the hell to do with me at this point. PO Bleucher stated, conveniently, that they were still completing their investigation, and made an appointment for me to see her again on July 17th, a Tuesday.

When I returned to the parole office on the 17th, I felt a strange sense that the atmosphere there was different somehow; there was an electric tension in the air, like something was afoot, and I imagined I was going to find out what the state planned to do with me now. My appointment time was very early, 8:00 AM, and that was rather unusual. Of course, I sat around waiting interminably for PO Bleucher to arrive, which occurred sometime after nine, although that was decidedly *not* unusual. We went into her office and talked for a short while, and then she said that she had to go out to make a phone call, and she would be right back. When she returned about 10 minutes later, she was accompanied by an armed deputy. I was charged with six counts of violation of parole against the State of Ohio, put into handcuffs and ankle shackles (ankle shackles! Can you say "overkill"?) and remanded to the Ashland County jail pending a hearing.

******

There is not a great deal to say about the run-up to my hearing, which finally took place toward the end of August, so I'll just hit the highlights. I would spend 38 days in Ashland County Jail while the wheels of justice grinded along as if they were infused with sand. However, I had already decided by the fifth day, perhaps even earlier, that I was not going to fight this, and I was going to make a request to the judge that I be sent back to Alaska to finish out, or flat-time, the remainder of my sentence in Palmer Correctional Center. (See Figures 3A through 3I at the end of this chapter.) I pled guilty to all six counts of parole violation, and I waived my right to be represented by an attorney, although I did consult with my lawyer before going in. He agreed with me, stating that there was really nothing he could do for me at this point, and I was grateful that he was good enough to be honest, and to save me a few bucks on what would have been wasted attorney fees.

I felt beaten and tired, but somewhat relieved that the ordeal of parole, at least, was over. In the court hearing, the judge had listened intently, and he seemed to understand my plight, though sympathetic as he might have been, he too, was powerless to do anything to help me. On August 24th I was turned over to two plain-clothed Alaska State Troopers who would escort me back to Palmer Correctional Center. I was not able to call my parents that day, presumably so that they would not be able to know when I was being moved, and thus could not come to the jail at the appointed time with tommy guns to "spring" me from jail. But in all seriousness, the Alaska troopers were extremely nice to me, one of them buying me two books at the airport in Columbus to read on the plane, and dinner for the three of us on a layover at Denver International Airport.

On the final leg of the flight from Denver to Anchorage, I thought about what my parents were going to do now, without having me around. I was concerned about them, despite the way they had treated me as their chief cook and bottle washer, houseboy and laundress, landscaper and all the rest. I was worried about dad's continuing heart and other health problems, and I felt bad about having to leave mom to deal with all of that on her own. I felt that by taking the action that I did, I had placed a great weight back on their shoulders. Notwithstanding, I had done what I felt in my heart I had to do, and when the plane touched down at Ted Stevens Anchorage Airport, I whispered to myself, "Home at last."

ADULT PAROLE AUTHORITY
I. Notification of Release Violation Hearing

TO:

Name:	Offender #/ICOTS #:	Date:
JERRY TANNER	IC209494	Jul 20, 2012
Location:	City:	State:
ASHLAND COUNTY JAIL	ASHLAND	Ohio

You are hereby notified that a Release Violation Hearing to determine whether or not you have violated the terms/conditions of your release will be held at (if you are being supervised under interstate compact the hearing is to determine whether or not there is probable cause that you violated the terms/conditions of your release):

Location:	Date:	Time:
ASHLAND COUNTY JAIL	Aug 7, 2012	10:00 A.M.

You have the following rights in regards to said hearing:

1. You may appear and testify on your own behalf;
2. You may present letters, reports, or other documentary physical evidence on your behalf, including evidence of mitigation;
3. You may request that persons who can provide relevant information be subpoenaed on your behalf;
4. You may confront and cross examine witnesses who testify against you, unless the Hearing Officer specifically finds good cause for not allowing confrontation;
5. You may seek disclosure of evidence presented against you;
6. You may request representation by counsel either retained by you or through the Ohio Public Defenders office if you meet the criteria set forth for such representation.
7. You may receive a written statement of the evidence relied upon to determine that you violated your release, and the sanction to be imposed.
8. You may request a continuance of the Release Violation Hearing.

If the Parole Board Hearing Officer or representative determines that you violated the conditions/terms of your release, he or she may revoke your release or impose a prison term sanction or other appropriate, less restrictive sanction.

If you are being supervised under interstate compact, it may be ordered that you be held in custody until State of Alaska determines whether to transport you to that state for a revocation hearing. That state may also order you to be released from custody and returned to supervision in Ohio or Alaska with sanction imposed.

DRC3304 B (Rev. 01/12)   DISTRIBUTION: VSP Officer, Unit, Jail/Reception Center, Offender   Page 1 of 4

FIG. 3A–D. My Notice of Violation Hearing and Plea Statement

You are alleged to have committed the following violation(s): 10/2009 Conditions   RULE 14

RULE 14. I agree to fully participate in, and successfully complete, the following indicated Sanctions/Special conditions: All orders of State of Alaska/Department of Corrections - General and Special Conditions of Supervision. "#3, Defendant shall secure the prior written permission of a probation officer of the Department of Corrections before changing employment or residence or leaving the region of residence to which assigned"

TO WIT: On or about 6/23/12 thru 6/25/12, you left your region of residence (Ashland County), without the prior written permission of your supervising officer.

Admit: [Initials] ✓   Admit with Mitigation: [Initials]   Deny: [Initials]

You are alleged to have committed the following violation(s): 10/2009 Conditions   RULE 14

RULE 14. I agree to fully participate in, and successfully complete, the following indicated Sanctions/Special conditions: All orders or state of Alaska/Department of Corrections - General and Special Conditions of Supervision: "#9, Defendant shall not consume intoxicating liquor."

TO WIT: On or about 6/23/12 thru 6/25/12, you consumed intoxicating liquor.

Admit: [Initials] ✓   Admit with Mitigation: [Initials]   Deny: [Initials]

DRC3304 E (Rev. 01/12)

FIG. 3B

You are alleged to have committed the following violation(s): 10/2009 Conditions   RULE 14

RULE 14. I agree to fully participate in, and successfully complete, the following indicated Sanctions/Special conditions: All orders of state of Alaska/Department of Corrections - General and Special Conditions of Supervision. "Special condition #5, The defendant shall not knowingly have any in-person contact with a person under 18 years of age unless in the immediate presence of another adult who knows the circumstances of his crime, and the defendant receives written approval by the Probation/Parole Officer for the contact to occur in the presence of the specified adult."

TO WIT: Between the time period of on or about June 2011 and June 2012, you had in-person contact with a 16 year old female, a 14 year old male and an 11 year old male without the written approval of your supervising officer.

Admit: [Initials: ✓]   Admit with Mitigation: [Initials:]   Deny: [Initials:]

You are alleged to have committed the following violation(s): 10/2009 Conditions   RULE 5

RULE 5. I will follow all orders verbal or written given to me by my supervising officer or other authorized representatives of the Court or the Department of Rehabilitation and Correction.

TO WIT: On or about 6/23/12 thru 6/25/12, you failed to comply with a written sanction, issued by your supervising officer requiring you not to leave your geographic area without the approval of your supervising officer.

Admit: [Initials: ✓]   Admit with Mitigation: [Initials:]   Deny: [Initials:]

FIG. 3C

You are alleged to have committed the following violation(s): 10/2009 Conditions RULE 5
RULE 5. I will follow all orders verbal or written given to me by my supervising officer or other authorized representatives of the Court or the Department of Rehabilitation and Correction.

TO WIT: On or about 6/23/12 thru 6/25/12, you failed to comply with a written sanction issued by your supervising officer requiring you not to consume any alcoholic beverages or enter any liquor establishments.

| Admit: | Initials: | Admit with Mitigation: | Initials: | Deny: | Initials: |

You are alleged to have committed the following violation(s): 10/2009 Conditions RULE 14
RULE 14. I agree to fully participate in, and successfully complete, the following indicated Sanctions/Special conditions: All orders of state of Alaska/Department of Corrections - General and Special Conditions of Supervision. "Special Condition #5, The defendant shall not knowingly have any in-person contact with a person under 18 years of age unless in the immediate presence of anther adult who knows the circumstances of his crime, and the defendant receives written approval by the Probation/Parole Officer for the contact to occur in the presence of the specified adult"

TO WIT: Between the time period of on or about June 2011 and June 2012, you had in-person contact with a 16 year old female, a 14 year old male and an 11 year old male and was not in the immediate presence of another adult who knew the circumstances of your crime.

| Admit: | Initials: | Admit with Mitigation: | Initials: | Deny: | Initials: |

Officer's Signature: ▓▓▓▓▓ Date: 7-23-12

I have read (been read) and understand the foregoing.

Offender's Signature: ▓▓▓▓▓ Number: IC209494 Date: 7/23/12

I certify that this notice was hand-delivered to the above on: Date: 7-23-12 Time: 1:25pm

Supervisor's Signature: ▓▓▓▓▓ Date: 7/23/2012

Inmate Number/ICOTS: IC209494 Inmate Name: JERRY TANNER

FIG. 3D

 # Waiver of Probable Cause Hearing/ for Interstate Compact Offenders Only

Name: JERRY TANNER

Date: 7-23-12

I have been notified of the violations of my release as served upon me on 7-23-12 .

I understand that I may waive my Probable Cause Hearing before a Parole Board Hearing Officer, or other authorized representative. In executing said waiver, I knowingly, voluntarily and intelligently waive the following:

1. The right to a personal appearance, and to present witnesses and/or documentary evidence on my behalf at a Probable Cause Hearing;
2. The right to confront and cross-examine adverse witnesses;
3. The right to representation by counsel.

Furthermore, I understand that by waiving a Probable Cause Hearing before a Parole Board Hearing Officer, or other authorized representative, and by admitting to one or more of the alleged violations that were served to me in the Notification of Release Violation Hearing, probable cause will be automatically established.

Furthermore, once probable cause is established, I understand I may be held in custody until the State of Alaska determines whether to transport me to that state for a revocation hearing. That state may also order me to be released from custody and returned to supervision in Ohio.

Initial: ✓

Waiver of Probable Cause Hearing / Interstate Compact Only

I hereby acknowledge that I have been advised of the alleged violations against me. I further acknowledge that I have read, and had read to me, my right to a probable cause hearing as well as my rights and responsibilities. I admit the alleged violations, and I hereby knowingly, voluntarily and intelligently waive my hearing. I further understand that I may be returned to Alaska , the sending state, for further revocation proceedings. I understand that by waiving my probable cause hearing and admitting to the alleged violations that probable cause is found.

Initial: ✓

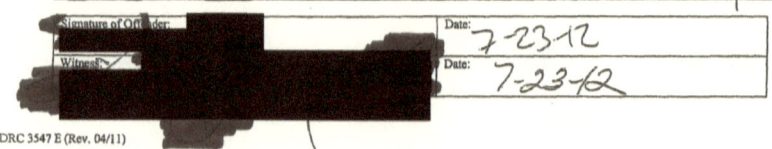

DRC 3547 E (Rev. 04/11)

FIG. 3E–F. My Waiver of Probable Cause Hearing

ADULT PAROLE AUTHORITY
II. Request for Witnesses

Name:	Offender #/ICOTS #:
JERRY TANNER	IC209494

I hereby request that the following witnesses/documents be subpoenaed to appear at my release violation hearing:

	Name/Document	Address	Information to be presented
1.			
2.			
3.			
4.			
5.			
6.			
7.			
8.			
9.			
10.			

[☒] I DO NOT request the presence of any witnesses/documents at my release violation hearing.

III. Notice of Counsel

[ ] I have retained the following counsel to represent me at my release violation hearing:

Counsel Name:
Address:
Telephone:

[ ] I request representation by the Ohio Public Defender Office at my release violation hearing.

[☒] I DO NOT request representation or counsel at my release violation hearing.

Offender Signature:	Date: 7-23-12
Witness Signature:	Date: 7-23-12

DRC 3309 (Rev. 05/09)

FIG. 3F

IN THE COURT OF COMMON PLEAS
OF ASHLAND COUNTY, OHIO

STATE OF OHIO,

    Plaintiff,

vs.

JERRY L. TANNER
LKA: 1434 Township Road 1353
       Ashland, Ohio 44805
DOB: 07-27-61
SSN: 296-60-0202

    Defendant.

Case No. 12-CRI-090

EXTRADITION COMPLAINT
Pursuant to Section 2963.11
ORC

    On or about August 3, 2012, in Ashland County, Ohio, Adult Parole Authority Officer ▓▓▓ received information that there was an outstanding warrant from the Superior Court in Palmer, Alaska, for Jerry L. Tanner. Jerry L. Tanner was at the Ashland County, Ohio Jail on an APA holder.

    The warrant was issued on July 20, 2012 in the Palmer County Superior Court, Alaska Case No. 3PA-509-316CR. The warrant is regarding the Defendant's failure to comply with conditions of probation based on a charge of Attempted Sexual Assault in the second degree. Authorities in Alaska have confirmed that the warrant is active and are willing to extradite the Defendant back to their jurisdiction for further proceedings on the warrant.

                                                        Complainant
                                             Adult Parole Authority

    SWORN to and subscribed before me by ▓▓▓ this 7th day of August, 2012.

                                           Deputy – Clerk of Courts

FIG. 3G. Extradition Complaint

WAIVER OF EXTRADITION

IN

2012 AUG -7 PM 3:31

The State of Ohio, Ashland County

Date: 08-07-12

ASHLAND, OHIO

I, **Jerry L. Tanner**, hereby certify that I freely and voluntarily agree to accompany authorities from Palmer, Alaska, as a prisoner of the State of Ohio, to the State of Alaska for the purpose of answering to the charge of failure to comply with conditions of probation pending against me in the Superior Court of Palmer, Alaska Case No. 3PA-509-316CR.

Furthermore, I hereby waive all formality and am willing to return to the State of Alaska without the Governor's requisition or other papers otherwise legal in such cases, and I hereby exonerate any and all person or persons from any blame of compulsion in this connection.

I hereby certify that the above agreement was signed by me in the presence of the undersigned and that it was made without any promise, threat or duress whatsoever.

Jerry L. Tanner

Witness

Witness

JUDGE, COMMON PLEAS COURT

JM # 60

FIG. 3H. Waiver of Extradition

IN THE COURT OF COMMON PLEAS
ASHLAND COUNTY, OHIO

2012 AUG 10 AM 10: 01

STATE OF OHIO,

    Plaintiff,

vs.

JERRY L. TANNER,

    Defendant.

Case No. 12-CRI-0▓▓▓

JUDGMENT ENTRY

This case came on for an extradition hearing on August 7, 2012. The State of Ohio was present in open court represented by Assistant Prosecuting Attorney ▓▓▓▓▓. The Defendant was present in open court not represented by counsel. The Court reviewed the right to counsel, including the right to court-appointed counsel, with the Defendant and the Defendant voluntarily and knowingly waived the right to be represented by counsel in this case.

The Defendant advised the Court that he wished to waive formal extradition proceedings and return voluntarily to the State of Alaska on the pending charge described in the Complaint. The Defendant also executed a written waiver of extradition. The Court accepted the wavier of extradition and orders it filed.

Based upon the Defendant's waiver of extradition and the Court's dialogue with the Defendant concerning extradition, it is hereby ORDERED that the Defendant shall be remanded to the Ashland County Sheriff's Office to await transport to Alaska authorities with regard to the pending warrant from that state.

It is so ORDERED.

JUDGE
COURT OF COMMON PLEAS

FIG. 3I. Extradition Order

CHAPTER 8
CONCLUSION

The Failure of the Promise of Parole and Probation as Vehicles of Reentry

The preceding and the primary narrative of this book is essentially a blow-by-blow description of one man's odyssey through the parole system of the United States, at least so far as within the guises of the states of Alaska and Ohio. It was my odyssey through the system, and it was a frustrating, insulting, demeaning, and often infuriating journey in which I was categorically prevented by the parole board and its officer representatives—and in my view and in actuality, prohibited through their tacit network of both internal and external strategies and tactics—from engaging in any remunerative work or business employment, business venture, or activity through which I might be able to put my life back together or to become a contributing member of society once again, all despite my earnest and sincere desire, and my numerous good faith attempts to do so against all the odds. In point of fact, I wanted nothing more or less than that. Yet the Departments of

Corrections in those two states used every imaginable means at their disposal to completely disrupt my daily life to make all of that a practical impossibility. And in fact, when the Department of Corrections in Ohio realized they could not stop me from doing something which I regarded as worthwhile, productive, and income-producing work by their usual methods of (a) imposing onerous and disruptive restrictions in the form of far-reaching "conditions of parole" that impact virtually every aspect of a person's daily life, (b) by forcing me to appear immediately at hastily and arbitrarily convened—and hastily and arbitrarily postponed and *re*-convened—meetings with parole officers or for polygraph tests, and (c) requiring me to take numerous alcohol abuse and sex offender classes or seminars, they resorted to something far more sinister and, by all the authoritative accounts or legal opinions that I know of or have been able to obtain, unequivocally illegal and unconstitutional.

That is, they stripped me of my basic constitutional rights as an American citizen, including the cornerstone right in our democracy to the Freedom of Speech. This was done here, in America, to one of its own citizens. In the end, I became so frustrated with the capricious, utterly dehumanizing, and in my view, the evil and self-serving behavior of the Department of Corrections of the State of Ohio, its parole board, and perhaps most of all, my parole officer, that I made the decision to waive a court hearing to determine my continued parole status and to instead be returned to prison to complete the remainder of my sentence, or flat-timing, as it's commonly referred to. That, I reasoned, was the only way to put an end, once and for all, to what I had come to realize first hand as the marginalized existence that defines life on parole in these United States. My experience taught me that when you are on parole in America, even in the 21st Century, you are, for all intents and purposes, a non-person.

1,825 DAYS OF HELL: ONE MAN'S ODYSSEY THROUGH THE AMERICAN PAROLE SYSTEM

Yet, if this is but one man's story, it is by no means an isolated one. Consider the following extract which opens perhaps the most definitive recently published scholarly assessment and critique of the efficacy—or more accurately, the lack thereof—of the role of parole in its stated purpose of facilitating the reentry of former convicts back into society as working, productive citizens in the community. Writing in 2011, Professor of Law, Criminology, and Criminal Justice Christine Scott-Hayward begins by quoting one such convict talking about his experience after being released on parole and endeavoring, essentially just as I had attempted, to get back to work:

> When I first came home, I was nervous. I didn't know what I was doing or which road to take. And then [parole] want[s] me to do all these appointments and all this other stuff.... It makes it even harder for one to be able to go out and get a job. You know when you have to be at an appointment at eight in the morning and they keep you there 'til eleven; then you know, you got a job interview at nine but parole is telling you, this is first, you can't do nothing about it (Scott-Hayward, 2011, p. 421).[1]

In her article, Scott-Hayward reported that more than 700,000 people were released from state and federal prisons in the United States in 2009, and that the vast majority of them faced significant challenges in reconnecting with family, finding

---

[1] Scott-Hayward, S.C. (2011). The Failure of Parole: Rethinking the role of the state in reentry. *New Mexico Law Review, 41*(2) Fall, 421–465.

housing and employment, and avoiding criminal behavior. She stated that for many people, "Reentry is further complicated" by the fact that "people released to parole are generally subjected to a large number of conditions, including regular reporting to a parole officer, avoiding police contact, submitting to drug testing, and finding and maintaining employment" (p. 421). Burke (2001) noted that "Although some conditions are clearly aimed at supporting the [individual] in transition, the total effect may be to create another layer of challenge to what is an already daunting situation" (p. 11, 13).[2]

However, other critics of the parole system go much further. Writing for *The Guardian*, Sadhbh Walshe points to the disturbing fact that probation and parole serve far more toward refilling American prisons and jails than they do to perform their other intended purpose of alleviating prison overcrowding, and thus these programs do more harm than good. She writes, "Parole and probation are intended as alternatives to incarceration for eligible offenders not deemed a threat to public safety.... But because the system (or, more accurately, lack of a system) is overburdened, underfunded and haphazardly managed, it frequently functions... as a feeder system, ensuring prison beds do not stay empty for long" (2012).[3]

Walshe goes on to cite the report compiled by the Pew Center for the States which found that parole violators accounted for over one-third of all prison admissions in the U.S. in 2005. It is important to point out here that a parole "violation" does

---

[2] Burke, P. (2001). Collaboration for Successful Prisoner Reentry: The role of parole and the courts. *Correction Management Quarterly, June*, at 11, 13.

[3] Walshe, S. (2012). Probation and Parole: A study in criminal justice dysfunction. *The Guardian*, April 26, 2012.

not necessarily indicate the commission of a crime. The Pew study concluded, among other findings, that "half the U.S. jail population is the consequence of failure of community supervision."

That may just be the tip of the iceberg, and in some states this problem has been documented to be far worse. In a New York Times article, writer Fox Butterfield (2003) described the state of California's parole system as a "one billion dollar failure." Fox cited a study conducted by a state watchdog agency known as the Little Hoover Commission—an independent, bipartisan agency appointed jointly by the Governor and the legislature—which concluded that a whopping "67 percent of those sent to prison in California were parolees being returned for violating a condition of their release." The Commission study found that California spent an average of $900 million annually to incarcerate parole violators and $465 million on supervising parolees, and that the bulk of the supervision costs were "for parole agents who spend much of their time filling out paperwork to send parolees back to prison" (2003).[4]

Butterfield reported that in the year or so prior to publication of the Little Hoover Commission study in California, 25 states had passed legislation aimed at reducing prison populations by reversing some of the tough mandatory sentencing laws of the 1980s and 1990s, as well as laying off corrections officers to close budget gaps. I would first point out that while the notion of making sentencing more reasonable (and moreover, that a democratic society ought absolutely to demand nothing less than balanced, fair-minded, and reasonable punishments for criminal convictions) in terms of "fitting the crime" is a

---

[4] Butterfield, F. (2003). Study Calls California Parole System a $1 Billion Failure. *The New York Times*, November 14, 2003.

noble and worthwhile goal in its own rite. Nevertheless, it has absolutely nothing to do with actively reforming the way our prison and parole systems actually operate after the conviction and incarceration of criminal offenders: It just means that you start off putting fewer people into the system in the first place, and I would certainly agree with the argument that many of the people who were sent to prison thanks to those "tough on crime," "three strikes you're out," mandatory sentences (for example, the so-called "Rockefeller Laws" in New York State) did not commit the types of crimes that deserved such severe punishments. However, and more pertinent to this discussion, simply reducing the number of people going into prison does nothing to reform the correctional system of incarceration for those who are actually already there or newly sent into it, nor does it necessarily do anything to help those placed on parole or probation once they get out of it.

But what is more telling are the reasons why, at the time of the Little Hoover Commission Study, the state of California, despite having the largest and most expensive prison systems in the nation, was one of the few states that had not acted to reduce corrections costs and, more importantly, to reform a clearly failing system that sent more people back to prison then it ever enabled to get out of the system, and presumably, back on their feet as productive members of the community and of society at large. Butterfield (2003) writes:

> A primary reason, experts say, is that the prison guards union, the California Correctional Peace Officers Association, is the most powerful union in the state and contributes the largest amount of any political action committee to politicians in the state. The union also represents parole

officers, and many of them began their careers as prison guards. Experts say the guards and parole officers have a financial incentive to keep the number of inmates high, helping preserve their jobs and ensure high salaries.

The numbers in California speak for themselves, as the state was not doing as good a job at preparing its inmates for release as it had done 20 years earlier: In 1980, about one in four parolees, or a total of 2,995 parole violators, ended up back in prison. In 2000, three out of four parolees were sent back, or a staggering total of 89,363 alleged parole violators!

In the foregoing, I have focused on California as the largest and most expensive correctional system in the country, thanks to the figures and conclusions provided by the Little Hoover Commission Study. For obvious reasons, few other states either have or are willing to openly provide such damaging hard data. However, there is absolutely no reason to believe that the situation is any different in any of the other 49 states or with the federal prison and parole systems. In fact, the national statistics clearly bear this out. They paint a picture of a so-called correctional system that is out of control and grossly dysfunctional, which I believe ought to both disturb and outrage every tax paying American. More critically, the current situation ought to alarm any freedom-loving Americans who believe in the right and liberties that are supposed to be guaranteed by the Constitution, but which are systematically being undermined and usurped by the very courts and departments of justice that are designed to preserve, protect, and uphold them. In the next section of this chapter, we look at the numbers compared to other countries around the world.

A Hard Look at U.S. Prison and Parole Statistics

One of the best ways to try to begin to grasp the sheer magnitude of the colossal failure of the correctional system in the United States is through a direct, apples-to-apples comparison with other countries around the world. The figures are both illustrative and mind-boggling, and I believe it bears repeating that they ought to be a matter of serious alarm and deep concern for all Americans who believe in a democratic society in which the basic rights embodied in our Constitution are sacrosanct and must be held inviolable at all costs. That picture is rapidly fading, and it gets even worse when we compare ourselves with countries that we so self-righteously deem to be totalitarian regimes, or even despotic ones, and which some groups in the U.S. would wish to indict for so-called human rights violations. Increasingly, this is a case of the pot calling the kettle black.

Let's compare the numbers. It is important to start by pointing out that all of the following data is taken from the latest information on the website of the International Centre for Prison Studies (ICPS), viewed in April of 2014.[5] The ICPS shares an academic partnership with the University of Essex in Great Britain. Most critically, ICPS works independent of any governmental or intergovernmental agencies; moreover, the organization is self-supporting and raises its own funding for all of its research and project activities. In light of these facts, I submit that it is reasonable to conclude that the Centre's mission to present objective and accurate data is clearly unbiased by any agenda, political, social, or otherwise.

---

[5] International Centre for Prison Studies (2014). www.prisonstudies.org, London. Viewed April, 2014.

According to the ICPS, the United States leads all the nations of the world with 2.23 million people incarcerated in our prisons and jails. That of course includes Russia, with a mere 674,100 prisoners, and while it should be duly noted that Russia's population is less than half that of the U.S., even doubling the number of prisoners in Russian jails still leaves the U.S. with nearly one million more prisoners than Russia. It also includes China with 1.7 million prisoners according to the ICPS, meaning that the United States has more than a half-million more prisoners than China, *a country with 1.3 billion people*, or four times that of the United States! That means by extension if the United States had the same population as China, we would have nearly nine million of our own people in prison![6]

Further, according to ICPS figures, the United States currently has a prison population rate of 707 prisoners per every 100,000 people in the population. Remarkably, that figure is actually down from some estimates not too long ago, when the rate was as high as 756 prisoners per 100,000 of population. Yet much of that decrease can probably be attributed to the easing of the oppressive and unreasonable mandatory sentencing guidelines of the so-called

---

[6] The ICPS adds the following caveat, stating that the figure of 1.7 million includes only sentenced prisoners: "The Deputy Procurator-General of the Supreme People's Protectorate reported in 2009 that, in addition to the sentenced prisoners, more than 650,000 were held in detention centres in China. If this was still correct in mid-2013 [the date of the last ICPS survey figures], the total prison population in China was more than 2,350,000." However, even if we include persons in China's detention centers—many of whom are most likely political prisoners–in the total prison population for China, this would still indicate that the U.S. has virtually the same total number of prisoners as China, a totalitarian regime with a population, as noted already, four times that of the United States.

"war on drugs" as previously mentioned. Nevertheless, the U.S. prison population rate in 1980 was closer to about 200 prisoners per 100,000 of population, or a whopping increase of nearly 330 percent over 30 years! However, by contrast, Russia's current prison population rate is 470 per 100,000. The rate in Iran, once an integral member of President Ronald Reagan's so-called "Evil Empire," is 284—*over 400 prisoners per 100,000 less than the U.S.!*

In a recent article posted on the Moyers & Company website, Joshua Holland (2013)[7] writes that, despite having only about 5 percent of the world's population, the U.S. houses 25 percent of its prisoners, making the U.S., quite arguably, the world's leading jailer, with more inmates than the top 35 European countries *combined*.

However, the statistics on parole and probation in the U.S. are even more staggering—and troubling. According to the U.S. Department of Justice Bureau of Justice Statistics (BJS), in 2004 there were nearly 5 million people on parole and probation combined (Glaze & Palla, 2005)[8]. Glaze and Palla (2005) further state in their report for the BJS that "Probationers accounted for half of the total growth in the correctional population since 1990.... Overall, the correctional population increased by nearly 2.5 million, or 57%, from 1990 to 2004" (p. 2). According to the authors, parolees and probationers accounted for 60 percent of that growth.

But here is the most disturbing statistic contained in the BJS report, and the one that is the primary focus of this book, which starkly points out the unconscionable failure rate of our correctional

---

[7] Holland, J. (2013). *Land of the Free? U.S. has 25 percent of the world's prisoners.* http://billmoyers.com/2013/12/16/land-of-the-free-us-has-5-of-the-worlds-population-and-25-of-its-prisoners/. Viewed May 2, 2014.

[8] Glaze, L.E., & Palla, S. (2005). *Probation and Parole in the United States, 2004.* Washington, DC: Bureau of Justice Statistics Bulletin.

system. Less than half—only 46 percent—of all parolees successfully complete parole without violating a condition of release, absconding, or committing a new offense. According to the BJS, over 200,000 parolees return to prison each year. Jacobson (2005) reports that nationally, parole violators account for about one third of all prison admissions, with a significant and sizable impact on the correctional department budgets of many states[9]. And the situation is getting worse by the day. Scott-Hayward (2011) states that, "In 2009, almost 730,000 people were released from state and federal prisons, an increase of more than 20 percent since 2000," and reports that "overall, 35 percent of admissions to state prisons in 2009 were for technical violations (p. 424, and 424, fn).

Why is this so? I believe that my own experience in the parole system, as described in detail in this book, goes a long way toward providing a disheartening and alarming answer to that question.

The Challenges to Reentry

Scott-Hayward (2011) identifies the several basic challenges that persons released from prison face when they return to the communities from which they came, specifically, as "reconnecting with family and peers, finding housing and employment, and more generally avoiding criminal behavior" (p. 421). And she acknowledges that this doesn't even begin to describe the complicated task of dealing with the gauntlet of requirements, restrictions, prohibitions, and the idiosyncratic demands and dictates of the poorly managed parole system, as well as the vagaries of its individual representatives. In my case, when I left

---

[9] Jacobson, M. (2005). *Downsizing Prisons*. New York and London: New York University Press.

Palmer Correctional Center I came home, essentially, to nothing. Because of my status as a convicted felon, I had been forced to sell or divest myself of the healthcare company I had founded, built from scratch—and loved. My family was 4,000 miles away. My life partner was gone, and, well, let's just say that, whether because of stigma or just the uncomfortable nature of the events that had transpired to create the situation I was in, not to mention the nature of the charges that were brought against me, it simply was not practical to associate with the friends that I had before all of that happened, beloved as they were to me.

For all of his other faults, PO Matthews through his own discretion allowed me to have contact with the "new" friends that I had made during my 16 months of incarceration. It would be nice to think that he did so out of some sort of even minimal compassion, perhaps from knowing the circumstances of my situation which had left me alone and isolated in America's most geographically massive and least densely populated state, but that, honestly, would be asking ludicrously too much. The fact is, he said it himself numerous times: he really didn't "give a shit" about who I talked to or associated with. Compassion, one may thus surmise, had nothing to do with it.

Housing

With respect to housing specifically, Scott-Hayward alludes to some of the formidable legal and social impediments ex-convict[10] parolees face when they are released from prison, citing

---

[10] The term "ex-convict," though I use it here, I have learned to be a misnomer. Because in America, as I found out, once convicted, you are always just a convict; you are never really an "ex" convict.

for example, "federal legislation passed in 1996 and 1998 [that allows] people with drug or violent felony convictions [to] be prohibited from living in public housing," and "an increasing number of landlords in the private sector [who] conduct criminal background screenings and decline to offer leases to people with criminal records" (2011, p. 426). As I noted in the narrative portion of this book, when I returned to Ashland, Ohio, I was obliged to move in with my parents despite the fact that I owned a perfectly good home of my own there, due to my status as a registered sex offender. And this aspect, too, points to the dysfunction of the DOC as well as its apparent confusion over its mission of facilitating reentry, in that one faction (the parole board) indicated that I could not live in the house due to its proximity to a small church day care facility, while another (the sheriff's office) said that I could live there. (Again, as I mentioned earlier, the sheriff's office would turn out to be right, but it would take frustrating and infuriating years to determine this, and by then it was too late, in that I had given up the fight and gone back to prison to flat time and get, once and for all, off paper with the state.)

Living with my parents again after so many years apart caused all of us in that house—and I would say especially me—an enormous amount of anxiety, stress and aggravation. Now, clearly the state of Ohio is not responsible for the "state" of the relationship between my parents and me, be it healthy or unhealthy. However, the removal or rescinding of my privacy rights by the state DOC effectively meant, for all practical purposes, the removal or rescinding of my parent's individual rights to personal privacy as well, as long as I was living in their home. Such that, for example, whenever my parole officer or other officials invaded my living space in order to check up on me, this also obliged them—and presumably to their way of thinking, *entitled* them—to barge into my family's home and to intrude on my parent's lives and personal space just as disruptively and upsettingly as they were doing to me. In this way, the DOC and its parole officers were directly responsible for heaping an enormous amount of additional stress onto what was already an excruciatingly stressful situation to begin with. And it was all completely unnecessary, as I learned when the sheriff's office finally decreed that I could have lived in my own home all along.

However, and much more importantly, what all of this dangerously suggests is that the power of the state to suspend, revoke, or otherwise ignore the constitutional rights of ex-convict parolees, such as the right of privacy and oh, so much more, extends to being able or permitted to as well suspend, revoke, or ignore the constitutional rights of the people around them, particularly those of their families and loved ones.

Finally, I want to add one last aspect with respect to the burden of suitable housing, though it is one that pales in comparison with the serious constitutional issues that I raise in this book. By refusing to allow me to live in the house on Center Street, the state also saddled me with the considerable financial and psychological burdens of dealing with a vacant property—paying the mortgage and taxes, paying for the maintenance and upkeep, the utilities—and trying to sell that property during one of the worst recessions since World War II, not to mention having to worry about possible eventualities like break-ins, vandalism, or other criminal activity that empty houses are often prone to. None of this, I would submit, was particularly helpful to my "reentry" into the community.

Employment

The second major challenge to successful reentry identified by Scott-Hayward is employment. However, I think that few people would disagree that gainful employment is probably *the* most crucial challenge of all. After all, if one can make enough money, one can certainly afford to fix any housing problems that one has. Scott-Hayward (2011) states that, "Research shows that there is a strong association between successful reentry and the ability to secure and maintain employment" (p. 426). That would seem to be self-evident, but she goes on to explain that former prisoners face significant barriers to obtaining employment, principal among them, of course, the plain fact of having a criminal record that will scare off many employers. But Scott-Hayward also notes the low education levels of the vast majority of former inmates, stating, "Most people enter prison with limited educational or vocational skills; a 2003 Bureau of Justice Statistics study found that about 40 percent of people in prison had not completed high school or its equivalent" (2011, p. 426–427).

Despite this fact, however, Scott-Hayward and others decry the fact that few inmates receive any sort of employment-related training, either while they are in prison or later, when they are on parole or probation. "Thus," she states, "Many people leaving prison lack the skills and/or qualifications to find work" (p. 427). Joan Petersilia, described by some as the preeminent scholar on parole and probation in the U.S., has criticized the abolition of Pell Grants to prison inmates, a ban which went into effect starting in 1994. Petersilia points out the deplorable reality that, because of the elimination of federal funding for college programs, between 1990 and 1997, the number of higher education programs in prisons decreased from 350 to eight (Petersilia, 2003).[11] That is nothing short of an outrage.

I can attest to this state of affairs first-hand. In my book, *Derailed*, I talked a great deal about the lack of training and educational opportunities for the inmates in Palmer Correctional Center, where in fact such programs were virtually nonexistent, so I will not go into great length on that aspect here, other than to say that I honestly felt very bad for these men who had little education and very few tools or skills for success once they got out of prison. And I will never forget that image, on the day that the PCC minibus summarily released me along with several other former inmates-cum-parolees in Anchorage, of those poor, pathetic souls wandering down the street, wide-eyed and bewildered, looking as though they had just been returned to Earth after having been abducted by aliens for several years, with no clue where they were going, or what they were going to do now. Predictably of course, as the statistics I have presented in this chapter bear out, most of them wound up back in prison.

But here's the interesting thing. Because in stark contrast to those men, I did have that precious formal education and the knowledge and skills to succeed on the outside, having attended Mansfield Business College and taken numerous college courses in business and finance ever since then. On top of that, in 1999 I had also gone to St. Alexis Medical Center in Bismarck, North Dakota, through an affiliate program with the University of St. Mary in Leavenworth, Kansas, for basic and emergency medical and paramedic training. I even taught EMS, EMT-I, EMT-II, ACLS, BLS, First Aid and CPR, and a few other things, for

---

[11] Petersilia, J. (2003). *When Prisoners Come Home: Parole and Reentry*. New York: Oxford University Press.

many years for the State of Alaska. On the other side of the coin, I could also make the solid claim that I have a prodigious resume of experience and "vocational" training in the "School of Hard Knocks," having successfully built two multimillion-dollar health care companies and employed hundreds of people. Certainly, if anyone was, I was as eminently qualified to find work as any recruiter or employer could conceivably ask for. However, none of that knowledge, education, training, or experience mattered. That is to say, none of that made any difference because it had nothing whatsoever to do with the reason—and there was *only* one reason—I was not able to find employment over the entire duration of the three years I spent on parole in Alaska and Ohio. That reason was, plain and simple: The Departments of Corrections in both states both prohibited and worked actively to prevent me from finding and/or undertaking any manner of employment or self-employment.

Now, I have throughout this book already described extensively and in great detail the considerable lengths to which these authorities went in order to actively prevent me from finding work, or from being able to maintain the kind of predictable, routine schedule that would be necessary if I was going to be able to successful in maintaining it, like any other good employee (or self-employed entrepreneur, for that matter). Indeed, I would submit that one could describe the narrative I have presented in these pages as a day-by-day historical account of the very campaign of anti-employment strategies and activities on the part of the authorities in question, much like describing, say, the war campaign and battle strategy of General Grant and the Union Army during the Civil War, just to cite a metaphorical example. So there is no need to reiterate or belabor the point here, except to say this: education and training or no, the department of corrections showed that they had absolutely no interest nor desire in seeing that I was able to successfully land a job, but was, quite to the contrary, much more interested in ensuring: (1) that I remained "in the system" for as long as possible, and (2) that my doing so, along with so much of the rest of the parole and probation population in America, further served to both justify and reinforce the need for their existence, and thereby preserve their jobs, as was noted earlier by Butterfield (2003). In this way I came to the realization that parole and probation in this country is a self-serving, self-propagating system of hypocrisy that has become, over the years, designed to feed on itself.

There is yet another important point to be made here. Estimates vary as to the number of parolees who return to prison due, not to criminal behavior or the actual commission of another new crime, but to nothing more than a simple parole violation, with some putting the figure at about 35 percent, while others put it much higher at about 45 percent. Scott-Hayward (2011) conservatively puts the figure at 35 percent, but seriously considers the sheer and frightening growth in the actual numbers themselves: "Between 1980 and 2001," she writes, "the number of parole violators admitted to prison increased from 21,177 to 215,450—*an increase of 917 percent!*" (Scott-Hayward, 2011, p. 437, emphasis added). Scott-Hayward goes on to state that this increase, "is one of the driving forces behind the overall growth in the prison population over the last thirty years, and is thus partially responsible for the fiscal crisis in corrections that is facing states today" (p. 437).

So, let's get this straight: We have these serious dual crises of prison overpopulation and of skyrocketing correctional department costs in large part because we place impractical, even impossible restrictions and onerous conditions of release on parolees, such that when they inevitably fail, we send them back to prison, and we hire hundreds and hundreds of parole and corrections officers to process the paperwork? Does this system make sense to *anyone*?

Further, I happen to be one of the people in that 35 percent statistic. I had committed no crime. I went back to prison rather than fight the charges of parole violations in court, only to win the Pyric victory of being granted the "opportunity" to be returned to what I had finally determined to be a wholly untenable and unacceptably unstable living circumstance—that of being a sort of trained monkey subject to the whim and fancy of the parole board and my various parole officers. And the fact is, owing to the vagueness and the overlapping nature of the conditions of parole themselves on the one hand (having to dance to the differing and sometimes conflicting conditions issued and enforced by two different states), and the accepted ability of parole officials to creatively interpret and enforce (or not enforce) such conditional sanctions independently, idiosyncratically, and illogically—again, according to their own whim—on the other hand, the fact is I could have been charged with a parole violation probably hundreds of times over the course of my three years on parole. For example, every time I might have walked down the street past a daycare center or a school (even if I didn't even know the center or the school was right there); every time I bought a sandwich in a deli that also sold package goods; every time I might have happened to be in the same room with an underage person—even if that person's parents were present, but did not "know the nature" of my crime—hell, every time I might have had a glass of wine with dinner at a respectable restaurant, and much more; I was at potential risk to be charged with a parole violation.

What had been the difference when such charges were actually formally brought against me? The answer, I submit, is as clear as the digital satellite and internet radio signal that would have carried my voice as a fully employed talk show host and personality, not to mention my words in print in books like the one you are reading. The DOC wanted to silence me, once and for all.

And finally on this point, if the other 55 to 65 percent of parolees who return to prison are indeed guilty of committing new crimes—a claim that I seriously dispute, and one that in my view is in serious need of independent investigation and more extensive study—given the barriers these people face, and the lack of remedial training or education to help them change, is it really any wonder that so many of them might resort to the only thing they might have known previously, which is of course, criminal activity?

A Corrupted System

Virtually everything that has been said here about the way that parole and probation systems presently operate, or are administered and overseen, stands in direct contradiction to their original intent and purpose. In her article, Scott-Hayward touches briefly on the origins of the concept of parole. She notes that in the U.S., parole was first instituted in 1876 at the Elmira Reformatory in upstate New York by its superintendent, Zebulon Brockway. Brockway implemented an indeterminate sentencing model along with parole release with the goals of both managing the prison population and, more importantly, preparing prisoners for release back into society. According to Scott-Hayward (2011), "Prisoners were classified based on their conduct, and after a certain period of good conduct, were released to the community while remaining under the authority of the correctional institution. For six months they were required to make monthly reports to a 'guardian' and these reports were sent back to the institution" (p. 431).

The crucial aspect that I want to make a point of here is that, as the author makes clear, the emphasis of the system was on rehabilitation as the primary goal of corrections. She cites a 1972 court case which defined the purpose of parole itself as "to help individuals reintegrate into society as constructive individuals as soon as they are able."[12] In most of the early parole systems in this country, supervision played a secondary role in the release decision process of the parole board. In other words, there was generally no active supervision of people on parole: parolees were expected to take on the responsibility of finding and maintaining a job as a means of getting back on their feet, and becoming productive members of society again. Parolees' responsibility to the board, or to their guardians, consisted of reporting in, usually monthly, and sometimes, as in the case of the early parole system in California, doing so simply by mail.

The upshot of this must be made clear. First, there was no legal power granted to the guardian to command or order parolees to report here or there on demand at a moment's notice; nor did the guardian have similar power to order parolees to attend substance abuse programs, or sex education classes, or the like. Parole boards and guardians similarly did not have the power to restrict the lawful movements of parolees in the course of their normal daily travels and activities—such as those which might actually be undertaken in the course of regular employment—and certainly did not have the power to tell parolees where they could and could not live! Instead, just to reiterate, parolees were held

---

[12] Morrissey v. Brewer, 408 U.S. 471, 477 (1972).

responsible to report in, presumably in writing for the most part, on a suitably regular basis or schedule.

Now, I will be the first to acknowledge that such a lenient and trusting approach probably will not work in our society today. However, I think it is important to point out that during my time on parole, I heard a great deal from each of my various POs about what "my responsibilities" were while I was still on paper with the state. Yet, those alleged responsibilities were always about my responsibilities *to them*—to the POs, to the parole board; my responsibility to appear at appointments, to go to classes or programs, and so on. It was never about any responsibility I had—indeed, responsibilities that I actually wanted—to get a job or to find safe and suitable housing—more particularly, my responsibility to myself, to my own self-respect, and by extension, my responsibility to earn back the respect and trust from my community by becoming once again an asset and a benefit to that community. And that's because of course, they really didn't want me to achieve those things, but rather, wanted me to remain beholden to the system that supports and preserves their jobs and livelihood, not to mention the massive government funding that supports the whole corrupt system.

Scott-Hayward then describes the political, social and legal machinations that significantly changed the system of parole, and the very nature of its focus, into the highly flawed system we have today, and which I argue is an utter failure and getting worse by the day. I do not have the space in this book to go into the details that have led up to the present degenerative situation, so I instead refer the interested reader to Scott-Hayward's excellent article in the New Mexico Law Review, which is available online.

Suffice it to say, however, that over the course of the latter half of the 20th century and continuing now in the 21st, the practical reality of the modern parole system has morphed into one of ever increasing surveillance by police authorities, reporting requirements, interventions and intrusions by authorities, disruptions of parolees' lives (as well as those of their families and loved ones), and gradual but unrelenting erosion and usurpation of basic constitutional rights, beginning most conspicuously with 4th Amendment rights to privacy and rights of association, but leading, as we have seen in my case, to undermining basic 1st Amendment rights to free speech, and finally, to greater and greater control over the individual person on parole. Scott-Hayward notes:

> While on parole, individuals have fewer privacy protections...are generally subject to searches and seizures without the Fourth Amendment requirements of probable cause or a warrant... special conditions may be imposed...to attend programs such as drug treatment or anger management [as well as] prohibitions on associating with particular individuals, and curfews. (p. 436)

The author attributes the growing and subversive dysfunction of the parole system to the radical changes in the overall supervisory style and strategy, pointing out that the system has evolved into much more of a managerial oversight and control model, and states further that under this system, parole officers look a lot less like social workers (or guardians) and a lot more like police or enforcement officers. Not surprisingly, as I have stated repeatedly in this book, all of these conditions and restrictions make the successful completion of parole much more difficult, to the point of unreasonable impracticality or even impossibility. As Jacobson puts it:

> Given all the social, economic, and health deficits of those coming out of prison, it becomes less than surprising that so many parolees are sent back to prison for rule violations. When one combines these problems with conditions that are routinely set for parole—no drug use, having a permanent address, having or actively seeking employment, keeping all reporting and treatment appointments—a recipe for failure results. (p.150)[13]

While I heartily agree with these statements, based on my own firsthand experience, I would argue that these assertions do not go nearly far enough: both authors have put the problem woefully mildly. Indeed, it is not a problem, it is a full-blown crisis, and it must be fixed. It is, after all and as I've said before, supposed to be the "department of corrections"; it is not supposed to be the "department of incarcerations."

---

[13] Jacobson, M. (2005). *Downsizing Prisons: How to reduce crime and end mass incarceration.* New York: New York University Press.

EPILOGUE

It's almost funny, in a cynical sort of way, but when I look back on my years on parole, I seem to have had some sort of thing going on with each anniversary of my release. It took almost exactly one year for my transfer to be approved, and while that was certainly not my fault, the singular, perhaps subliminal epiphany I had within days, even hours, of setting foot in Ohio was that this might be a colossal mistake for all of the reasons that I've already detailed earlier in the book. Then on my second anniversary, my decision to "go out drinking" to celebrate resulted in a relatively minor car crash, though sufficiently serious for the "cutting edge" technological wizardry of my 21st century automobile to rat me out to the police, which meant more courts, fines, lawyer expenses, Mickey Mouse substance abuse classes, and psychological counseling—and more depression. Then for an encore, only a few days before my third anniversary, I committed a serious parole violation that sent me back to Palmer Correctional in Alaska, though I would have to spend 39 days in the Ashland County jail while I waited for that slow motion axe to fall.

The title of this book—"1825 Days of Hell"—is something of a misnomer, in that what I have described in its pages is largely confined to my time on parole, from my release from Palmer Correctional Center on June 28, 2009 to my return there on

August 24, 2012, or roughly 1,121 days of hell, give or take. The remainder of the days, of course, consisted of the two separate stays in PCC, punctuated as they were by my three years on parole. I already described prison life in some detail in my first book, *Derailed,* so again, there is not much to add about my time in "the big house." The only thing left to say about that experience amounts to yet another irony, which didn't really hit me until I went back for the second time.

Specifically, in my first stint as a guest of the State of Alaska and an inmate of PCC, I worked for the prison supply and shipping department, eventually handling all of the purchasing, invoicing, and inventory processing. I managed several budgetary accounts, keeping prison officials informed as to when those accounts needed to be replenished, and generally making sure they stayed within their budgets, and all for the stunning salary of upwards of a dollar an hour. Basically, I told them what they needed, what they could afford to buy and when they could buy it. You might say that for a time I was the Milo Minderbinder of PCC, although I never did get my hands on any Egyptian cotton. When I went back for my second stay behind prison bars, I worked as a tutor in the prison's education department, helping many of the other inmates who had never graduated high school to take courses and earn their GEDs. That, by the way, was the full extent of education and training that was available to the inmates inside PCC.

So the plain fact of the matter is that I was actually more "employable" when I was locked up in prison than I was when I was out "free" on parole! I believe there is a distinct and disturbing reason for this. I have said all along that the ultimate goal of the Departments of Corrections, parole boards, and parole officers is control. And nowhere did these authorities have more control over me and my activities than when I was in prison. Therefore, they could afford to let me work while I was inside, where they could thus observe and effectively control every single thing that I did, whereas on the outside, conversely, they could not do that quite as easily. Or at least, it was a lot more difficult for them to do so. And that's not even to mention that if I succeeded on the outside, they stood the risk of "losing me" as one of the charges they were duly sworn to oversee and "keep in line," and from whom to "keep the public safe."

If all of that sounds like I am making too much of the attitude and policy disparity between prison and parole, or even if you find it even remotely ridiculous to make such a comparison, I would argue that it may be much more revelatory than it appears on the surface. Because it serves to highlight, I believe, the stark contrast between the rehabilitative interpretation of the function of departments of corrections as originally conceived in the past, with the high-surveillance, conditionally restricted, and highly constrained strict-control managerial model (to use Scott-Hayward's term) that has replaced it today, with incarceration being of course, the ultimate vehicle of managerial control. That, I submit, is why more parolees wind up going back to prison than successfully complete a program of parole. The hypocrisy of the system is evident in what I said at the conclusion of the research chapter (8) of this book: It is supposed to be the department of corrections, not the department of incarcerations.

www.ingramcontent.com/pod-product-compliance
Lightning Source LLC
Chambersburg PA
CBHW032016170526
45157CB00002B/718